BIVARIATE DATA

NCEA Level 3 Internal

Charlotte Walker and Victoria Walker

Walker Maths 3.9 Bivariate Data
2nd Edition
Charlotte Walker
Victoria Walker

Cover design: Cheryl Smith, Macarn Design
Text design: Cheryl Smith, Macarn Design
Content manager: Siew Han Ong

Acknowledgements
Cover photo courtesy of Shutterstock.

We wish to thank the Boards of Trustees of Darfield and Riccarton High Schools for allowing us to use materials and ideas developed while teaching. Our thanks also go to all past and present colleagues, especially Kath Wilson, who have generously shared their experience and ideas.

For product information and technology assistance,
in Australia call **1300 790 853**;
in New Zealand call **0800 449 725**

For permission to use material from this text or product, please email **aust.permissions@cengage.com**

National Library of New Zealand Cataloguing-in-Publication Data
A catalogue record for this book is available from the National Library of New Zealand.

978 0 17 046229 7

Cengage Learning Australia
Level 7, 80 Dorcas Street
South Melbourne, Victoria Australia 3205

For learning solutions, visit **cengage.co.nz**

Printed in China by 1010 Printing International Limited.
0 7 25

CONTENTS

Glossary

Make your own glossary of key terms:

Term	Definition	Picture/Example
Multivariate data		
Bivariate data		
Discrete variable		
Continuous variable		
Descriptive variable		
Sample		
Population		
Inference		
Response variable		
Explanatory variable		
Regression		

 ISBN: 9780170462297

Term	Definition	Picture/Example
Regression line		
Correlation		
Causality		
Interpolation		
Extrapolation		

What is statistical inference?

Statistical inference is the process of analysing sample data and suggesting what one might see in the population.

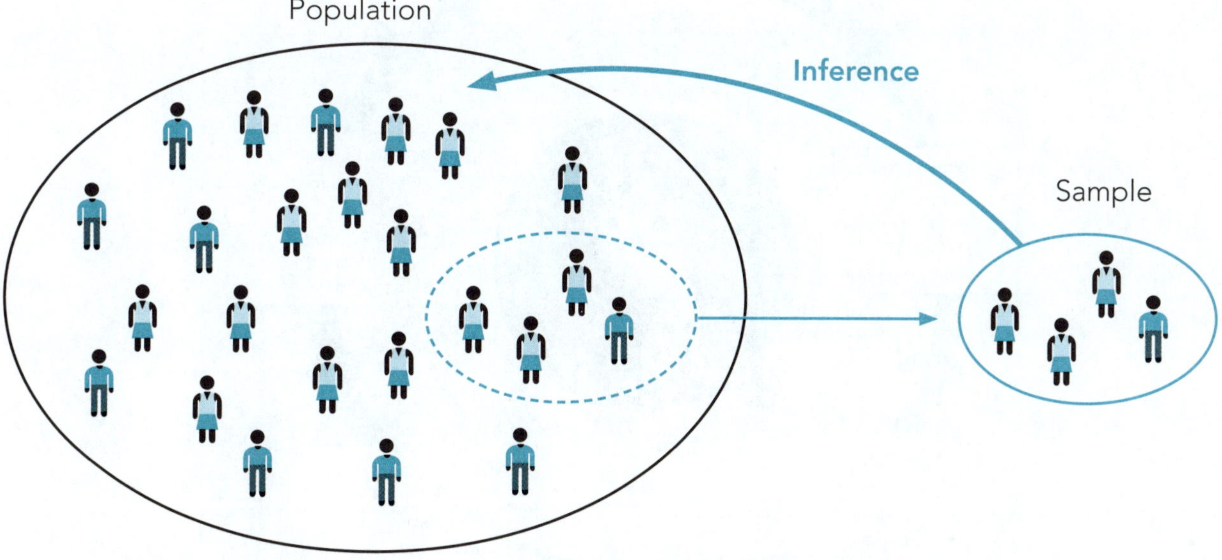

For bivariate investigations, this means looking beyond the sample and making a suggestion about a population.

ISBN: 9780170462297

Introduction

This standard will require you to investigate relationships (if any) between sets of data. It states you will be required to:

- From a multivariate data set, pose an appropriate **question** which is informed by contextual knowledge
- Select and use appropriate **displays**
- Identify **features** in the data
- Fit an appropriate **model**
- Describe the **nature and strength of the relationship**, and relate this to the context
- Use the model to make a **prediction**
- Answer the question and communicate findings in a **conclusion**.

What is bivariate data?

- This is where you have **two** pieces of data from each member of the sample or population, e.g. a child's height and weight.
- You analyse **both at once** to see if there is a relationship between them.
- Each pair of values is **plotted** as a point on a **scatter** graph.
- The explanatory variable may be discrete or continuous but the response variable **must** be continuous.

Statistical enquiry cycle

Your report should connect back to all aspects of the statistical enquiry cycle:

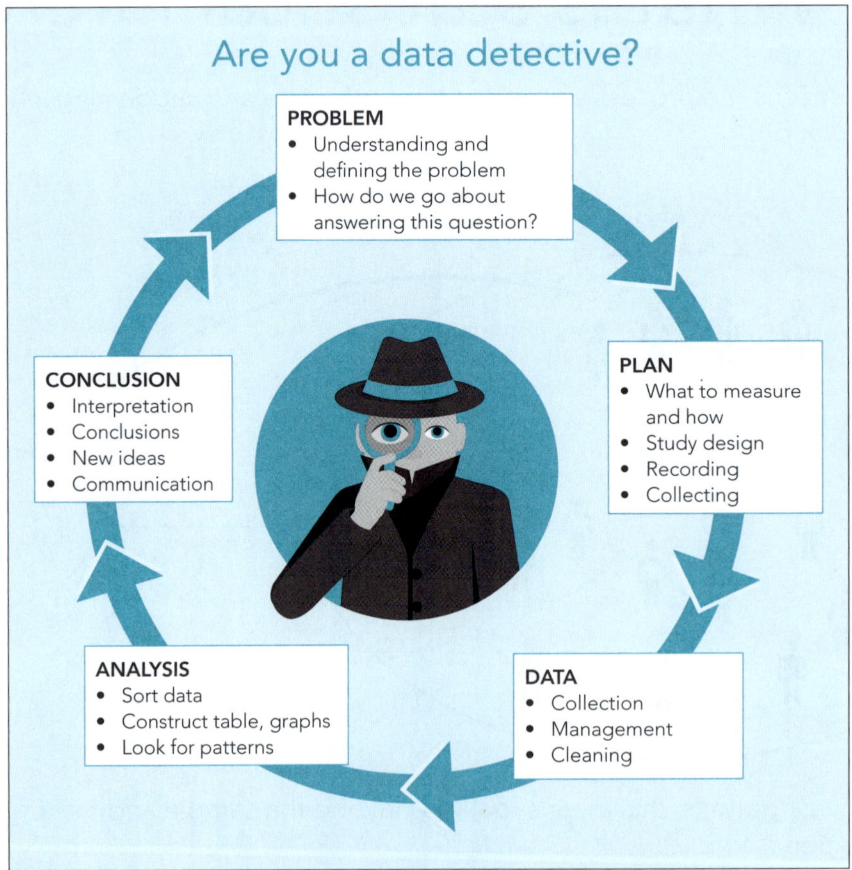

 ISBN: 9780170462297

Variables

There are three types of variables:

Continuous variables These are **measured** values, which can be **fractions or decimals**. Examples: height, weight, distance, time.

Discrete variables These are **counted** values, which are usually **whole** numbers. Examples: number of pets, shoe size (although this is unusual because these can be in halves).

Descriptive variables These are **categorical** variables, which are usually **words**. Example: eye colour, type of pet.

In theory we should analyse only continuous bivariate data. However, in practice, provided there is a large enough range, we sometimes analyse bivariate discrete data as the explanatory variable, e.g. marks out of 100.

Complete the table by stating what type of variable each is, and whether or not (✓ or ✗) each would be a suitable as the response variable in a bivariate study.

Variable	Type of variable	Suitable for a response variable?
Favourite colour	Descriptive	✗
Foot length		
Number of pens in students' pencil cases		
Head circumference		
Clothing size (XS, S, M, etc.)		
Number of pets per family		
Number of text messages on students' phones		
Favourite ice-cream flavour		
Height		
Size of your bedroom (m^2)		
Distance travelled to school		
Eye colour		
Arm span		
Make of calculator		
Age		

From the list, select some pairs of variables that would be suitable for a bivariate investigation.

	and	
	and	
	and	

ISBN: 9780170462297

Requirements of a basic report

You must:

1 Research your context.
2 Select suitable data — select two appropriate variables from a multivariate set of data.
3 Pose an appropriate question informed by contextual knowledge.
4 Name the response variable, name the explanatory variable, and justify your choice.
5 State the purpose of your investigation and who might find it useful.

Example:
The results of a fishing competition held during one day in the Marlborough Sounds are shown in the table on the opposite page. For each boat entered, the following are recorded:

- Boat name.
- Boat length: in metres.
- Species: the species of the longest fish caught.
- Fish length: the length of the longest fish caught (rounded to the nearest cm).
- Fish mass: the mass of the longest fish caught in kg (rounded to 2 dp).
- Age of catcher: the age of the person who caught the longest fish.
- Number of species caught: the total number of different species caught from each boat.

Blue cod

Kahawai

Kingfish

Snapper

ISBN: 9780170462297

Boat name	Boat length (m)	Species	Fish length (cm)	Fish mass (kg)	Age of catcher (years)	Number of species caught
Agatha	3.5	Snapper	67	5.56	17	1
Miss Jenna	7.2	Kahawai	55	2.10	39	3
Kotare	7.6	Blue cod	55	3.30	62	3
Heavy Metal	11	Blue cod	42	1.77	70	5
Wakanui	22	Kahawai	60	3.11	83	6
Kokiri	5.6	Snapper	39	1.28	44	2
Waiata	6.9	Snapper	47	1.90	56	3
Taranui	13	Blue cod	53	2.23	26	5
Crazy Cat	12	Snapper	45	1.82	11	1
Obsession	9	Blue cod	39	1.00	25	3
Takapu	18.7	Blue cod	51	2.05	45	2
Moana	4.8	Snapper	38	1.06	62	2
Endless	7.1	Snapper	48	1.93	51	2
Hapuku	7.6	Snapper	47	1.88	49	1
Happy Daze	9.3	Blue cod	41	1.10	38	4
Abigail	15.2	Kahawai	82	6.65	81	5
Reeltime	15.3	Snapper	62	4.31	20	2
Barracuda	6.1	Snapper	40	1.29	77	1
Mephistopheles	14.5	Blue cod	54	2.75	19	2
Ernie	3.8	Snapper	41	1.42	34	1
Kuaka	4.9	Kahawai	42	1.21	44	4
Taniwha	11.2	Blue cod	44	1.96	16	4
Albatross	10.1	Snapper	49	2.38	15	3
About Time	16.5	Blue cod	50	2.10	26	3
Windsong	19.4	Snapper	64	5.11	64	2
Ocean Dancer	7.9	Blue cod	44	1.94	39	4
Ariel	9.8	Kingfish	65	3.90	28	4
Toroa	8.1	Blue cod	47	1.60	32	3
Celine	17.8	Kingfish	88	8.51	60	3
Footloose	9.3	Snapper	58	3.56	38	2
Torea	3.2	Kahawai	40	1.51	19	1
Impulse	16.6	Kahawai	66	3.72	69	4
Enigma	6.8	Blue cod	38	1.08	34	6
Aoraki	9.7	Kahawai	62	3.59	37	3
Tenacity	11.9	Kingfish	83	6.90	8	3

ISBN: 9780170462297

1a Research your context

- Any statistical analysis should be undertaken alongside research and relevant contextual knowledge.
- The purpose and question for your analysis need to be informed by this contextual knowledge.
- You must reference your research. Be careful to use legitimate websites.

What information would you need to know/research before using the data set on page 9?

____

____

____

____

____

____

1b Select suitable data

- Most graphing programs will produce an appropriate graph if suitable variables are selected.
- You need to select at least two variables.
  1. The variables must be suitable for a **scatter** plot.
  2. The variable on the **y-axis must be continuous**. The variable on the *x*-axis can be either discrete or continuous.
  3. The variables should be **interesting** to analyse and research.

Note: Consider a reason someone might want to predict the response variable from the explanatory variable. This will help to identify a meaningful purpose.

Identify whether the variables in these graphs are suitable for bivariate investigation and give reasons if they are not.

1

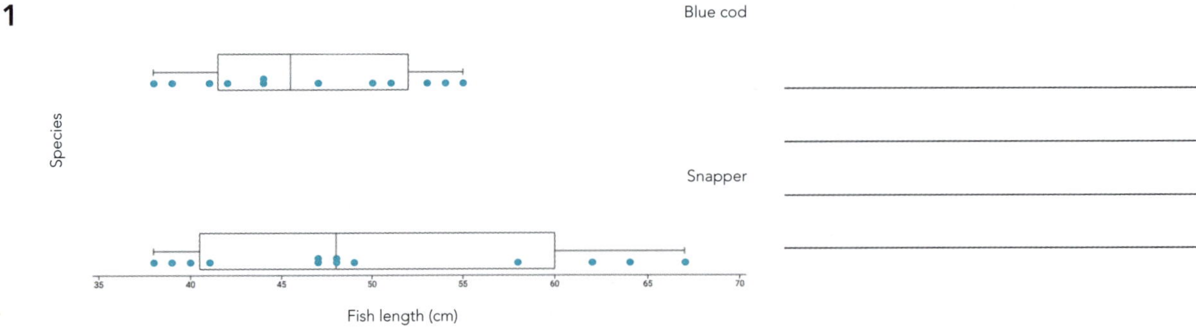

____

____

____

____

ISBN: 9780170462297

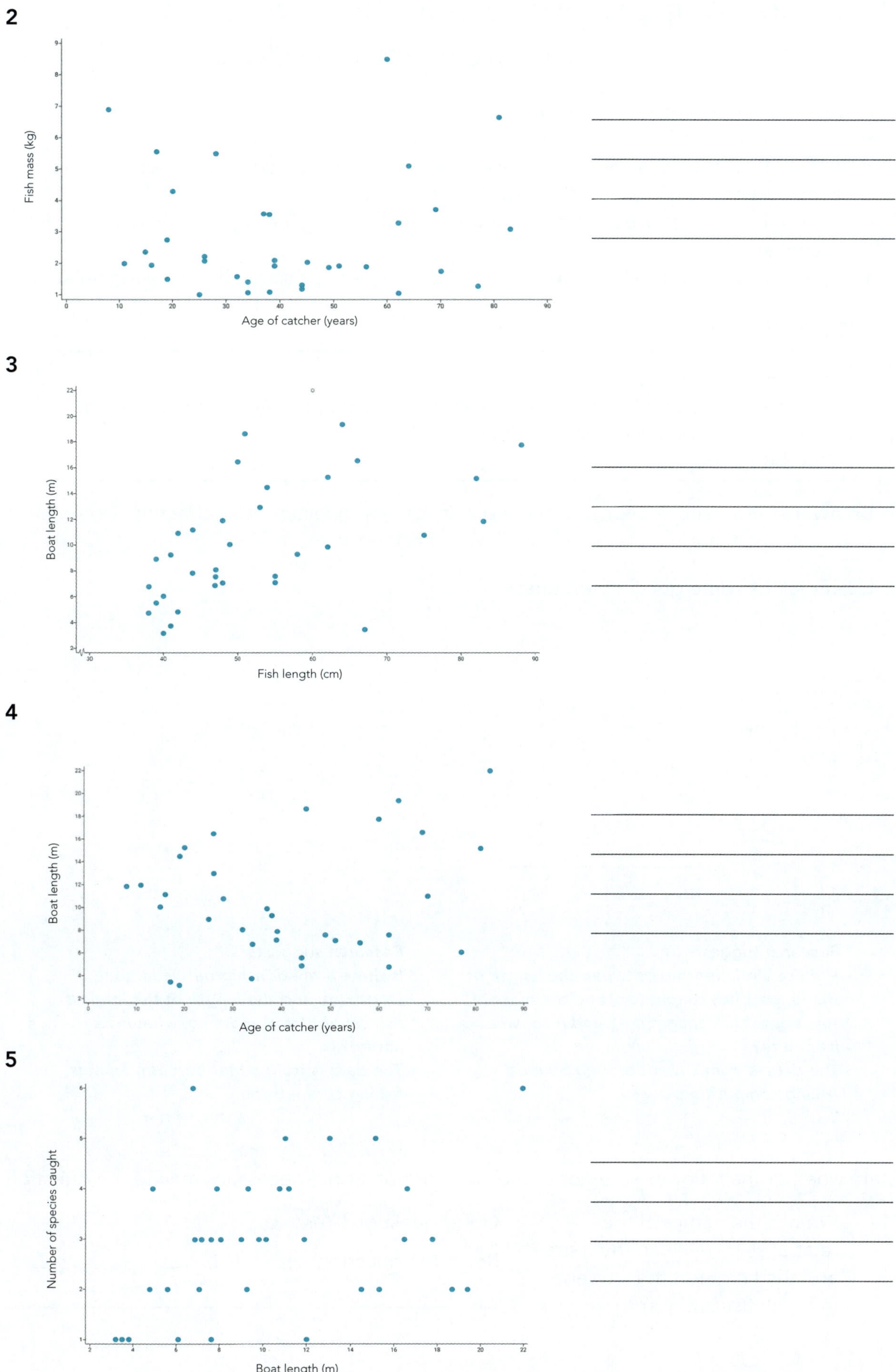

ISBN: 9780170462297

2 Pose an appropriate question which is informed by contextual knowledge

Features of an appropriate question:

- It should include details of **units** and **context**.
- It should **not** just have yes or no answers, e.g. 'Is there a relationship between A and B?'
- It should **not** imply that there is a relationship.
- It should lead to **interesting mathematical analysis**, e.g. fitting of a curve, unusual points, etc.
- It should have **scope** for research, discussion and perhaps suggestions for further study.

Suggested format:

> **Research suggests ...**
> **Is there a relationship between (variable on *x*-axis (units)) and (variable on *y*-axis (units)), and if so, what is its nature?**
> **The data is from ...**

Be aware: Your choice of data and the quality of your question may affect the potential depth of, and therefore the standard of, your final report.

Examples of some good questions:

1

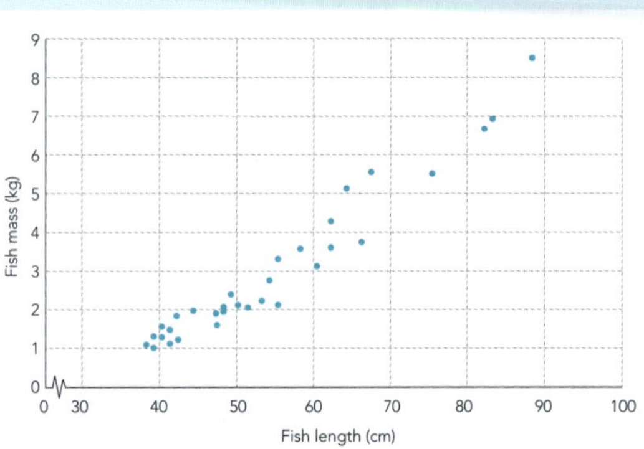

Research suggests ...
Is there a relationship between the length of the longest fish caught (cm) and the mass of the longest fish caught (kg), and if so, what is its nature?
The data is from a Marlborough Sounds fishing competition.

2

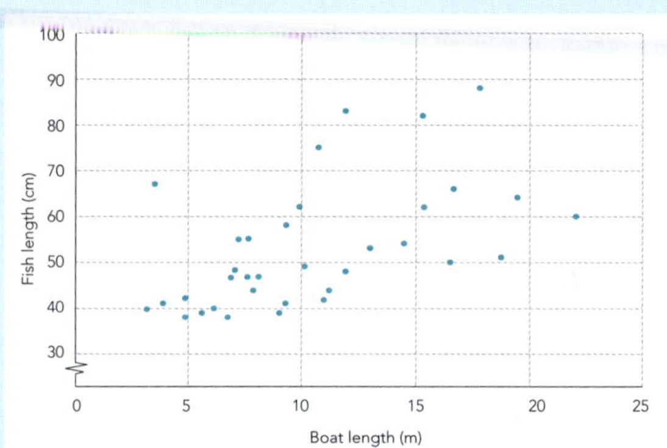

Research suggests ...
Is there a relationship between boat length (m) and the length of the longest fish caught (cm), and if so, what is its nature?
The data is from a Marlborough Sounds fishing competition.

State whether the following are good questions or not, and if necessary, rewrite the question.

1 What is the nature of the relationship between the mass and the height of the students in my statistics class?

Good question? Yes/No

Rewritten question: ______________________

____

____

ISBN: 9780170462297

2 Is there a relationship between leaf length and leaf width for rewarewa trees, and if so, what is its nature?

Good question? Yes/No

Rewritten question:____________________

3 Does the amount of fertilisier (g) given to each tomato plant in my garden affect the mass (kg) of tomatoes produced by each plant?

Good question? Yes/No

Rewritten question:____________________

4 Is there a relationship between the age of a brown kiwi chick (days) and its mass (g), and if so, what is its nature? The data is from a Kiwi sanctuary in the Wairarapa.

Good question? Yes/No

Rewritten question:____________________

Write appropriate questions to match the following graphs of data.

5 This data is from students at Mansfield University.

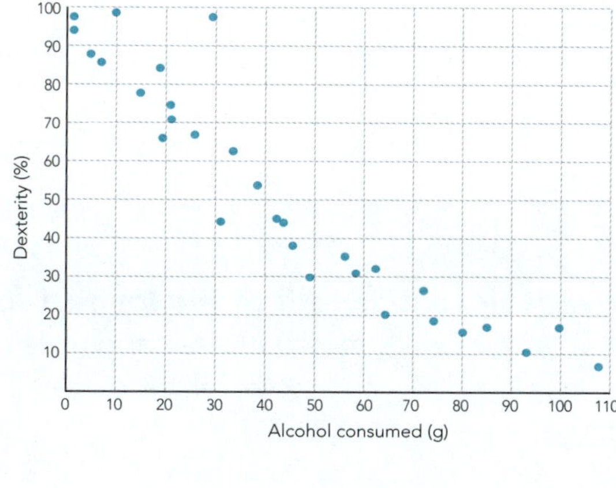

6 This data is from a day walk completed by members of Humphrey's tramping club.

Time taken (minutes)

100 90 80 70 60 50 40 30

0 10 20 30 40 50 60 70 80

Age of walker (years)

ISBN: 9780170462297

3 Name the response variable and the explanatory variable, then justify your choice

Explanatory (independent) variable:
- is plotted on the **x**-axis
- may partly **explain** the changes in the response variable
- can sometimes be **controlled** in an experiment
- may be the variable that is most easily measured in order to estimate the response variable
- **may** be **continuous** or **discrete**.

There may be **several** explanatory variables that contribute to the response variable.

Response (dependent) variable:
- is plotted on the **y**-axis
- is the **focus** of our question
- is the variable that we want to **predict**
- **measures** the outcome of a study
- **must** be **continuous**.

There is usually just **one** response variable.

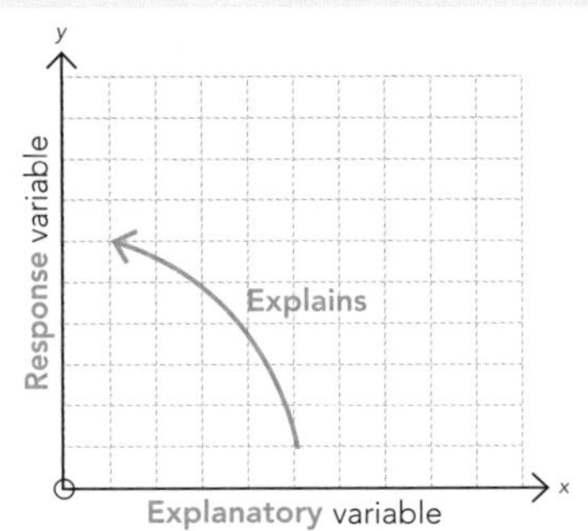

Example:

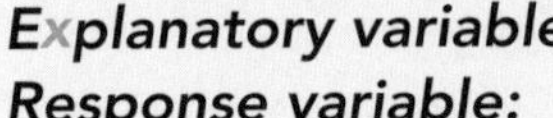

Is there a relationship between boat length (m) and the length of the longest fish caught (cm), and if so, what is its nature?

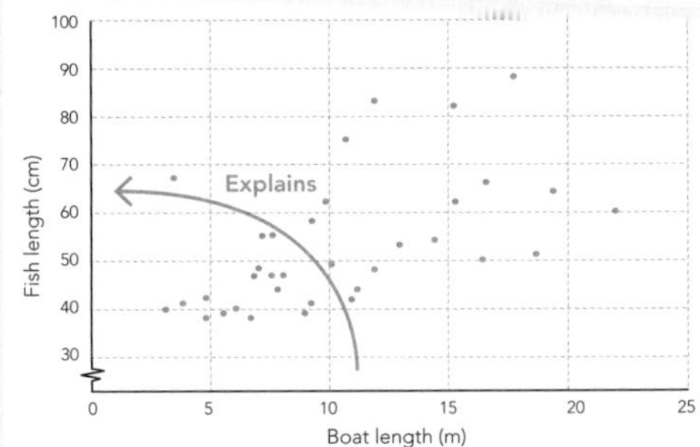

Explanatory variable:	*boat length (m)*
Response variable:	*length of longest fish caught (cm)*

Reason:
I have chosen boat length ***as the explanatory variable, and length of the longest fish caught to be the response variable****. I think that larger boats may be faster and able to access better fishing areas. Also, larger boats can hold more people, which might increase the probability of catching bigger fish.*

How this information could be used:
It could be useful to be able to predict the length of a fish by the length of the boat to see if there is an advantage in having a bigger boat. In future fishing competitions, it might be fairer to have categories for different sizes of boat.

Note: Sometimes either variable could be classified as explanatory or response — particularly in observational studies. When this happens you can have either variable on the x-axis. You should justify your choice.

ISBN: 9780170462297

State which is the explanatory and which is the response variable, and write each variable on its appropriate axis. You may wish to discuss these with your class.

1 Plant height: ______

Amount of fertiliser applied: ______

Reason: ______

______

______

How this information could be used: ______

______

2 Age of car: ______

Value of car: ______

Reason: ______

______

______

How this information could be used: ______

______

3 Depth of river: ______

Amount of rainfall: ______

Reason: ______

______

______

How this information could be used: ______

______

4 Temperature: ______

Plant growth: ______

Reason: ______

______

______

How this information could be used: ______

______

ISBN: 9780170462297

5 Size of stoat population: ______

Time spent stoat trapping: ______

Reason: ______

How this information could be used: ______

6 A child's reading ability: ______

A child's age: ______

Reason: ______

How this information could be used: ______

7 Length of a tramping track: ______

Time taken to walk it: ______

Reason: ______

How this information could be used: ______

8 Profit of ice creams sold: ______

Air temperature: ______

Reason: ______

How this information could be used: ______

ISBN: 9780170462297

4 State the purpose of your investigation and who would find it useful

- You need to justify **why** you have chosen your two variables.
- You need to discuss **who else** might be interested in your investigation.
- Do **not** discuss what you see in your graphs at this stage.
- Discuss any **prior research** you have done and include **references**.

Examples:

1 Is there a relationship between the length (cm) of the longest fish caught and its mass (kg), and if so, what is its nature?

Why might we investigate this:
I would like to know if longer fish are heavier. It seems fairly likely that they will be. A strong relationship would mean that during competitions, fish could be photographed on a standard measure to show their lengths. Then they could be released unharmed. It may mean that the organisers of fishing competitions need to record either the weight or the length of fish, not both.

Who might be interested:
Organisers of fishing competitions. Also, the relationship for any particular species might tell fisheries management about the health of the fish population.

2 Is there a relationship between boat length (m) and the length of the longest fish caught (cm), and if so, what is its nature?

Why might we investigate this:
I would like to know if longer boats catch bigger fish. In some parts of the world there is evidence that big boats cannot catch the big fish because they can't get into the shallow waters where the big fish live (www.discoverboating.com/resources/article.aspx?id=399). In New Zealand some of the species caught in this competition do live in very shallow water at times (e.g. snapper: http://www.nzfishingworld.co.nz/latest/2015/08/shallow-water-snapper). However, all of the species caught in this competition are usually caught at depths which are accessible to big recreational boats, but which may not be accessible to smaller ones. (https://issuu.com/thefishingpaperonline/docs/2015_marlfishguide_issuu).

Bigger boats can probably safely access areas that are not fished as frequently, which could also give them an advantage. It would be interesting to find out where the longest fish were caught. However, I think one of the major factors might be that big boats can hold more people to do the fishing, and this must increase the probability of catching a big fish. It would be interesting to know how many people were fishing from each boat.

Who might be interested:
The organisers of this competition should be interested in this investigation. If bigger boats catch bigger fish, they might consider introducing a handicap for bigger boats in the future. Otherwise they might consider different categories for different boat sizes. Also, those involved in fisheries management might be interested. Perhaps they might consider different rules for bigger boats.

Notice that, even though the relationship may not be as strong, the second 'question' leads to more interesting discussion opportunities than the first.

ISBN: 9780170462297

Discuss why we might investigate the following questions, who might be interested and what you might research.

1 Is there a relationship between the age of a walker (years) and the time it takes to walk a track, and if so, what is its nature?

Why might we investigate this:

Who might be interested:

What might you research:

2 Is there a relationship between the gestational time (weeks) and the mass of the baby (g), and if so, what is its nature?

Why might we investigate this:

Who might be interested:

What might you research:

ISBN: 9780170462297

5 Select and use appropriate displays

- Your graphing program will produce a scatter plot for you, as long as you choose suitable variables.
- You may have to add or modify:
  1 The **title**
  2 The **axis labels**, including units.

Example:

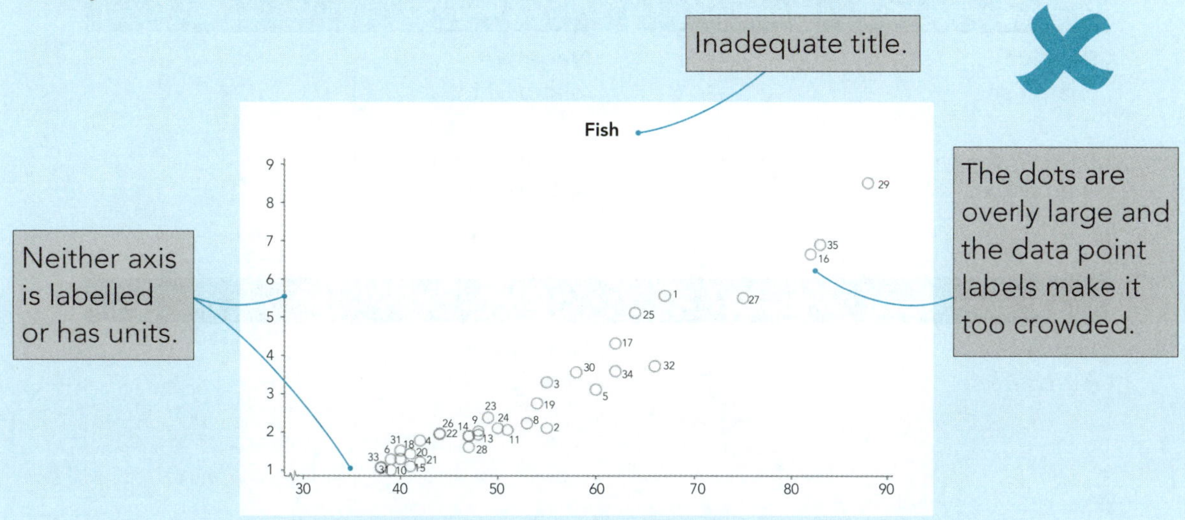

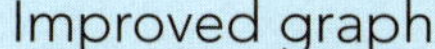

Improved graph:

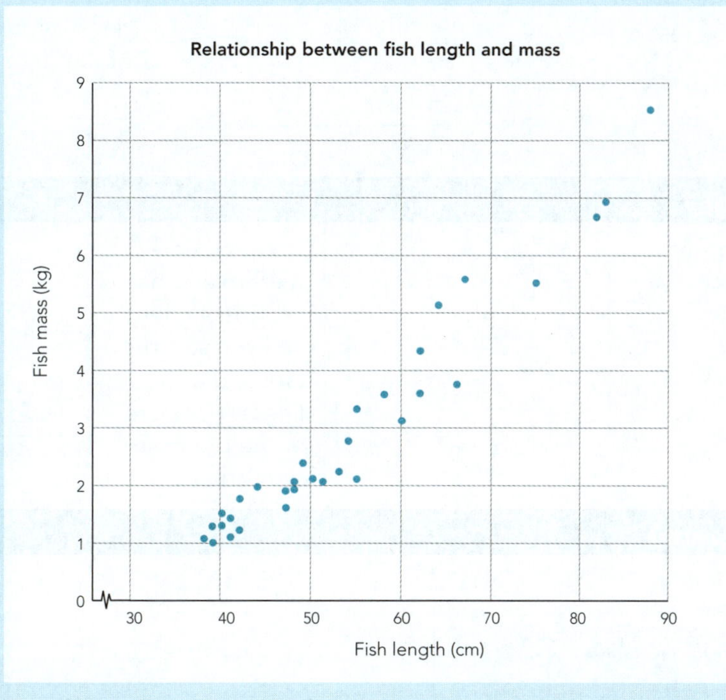

6 Identify features in the data

- You need to write a **general** description of the data, and identify the features. This should be done before adding a trend line.
- Later in your report you should discuss each of these in **more detail**, and relate them to the context.

Features you should look for:

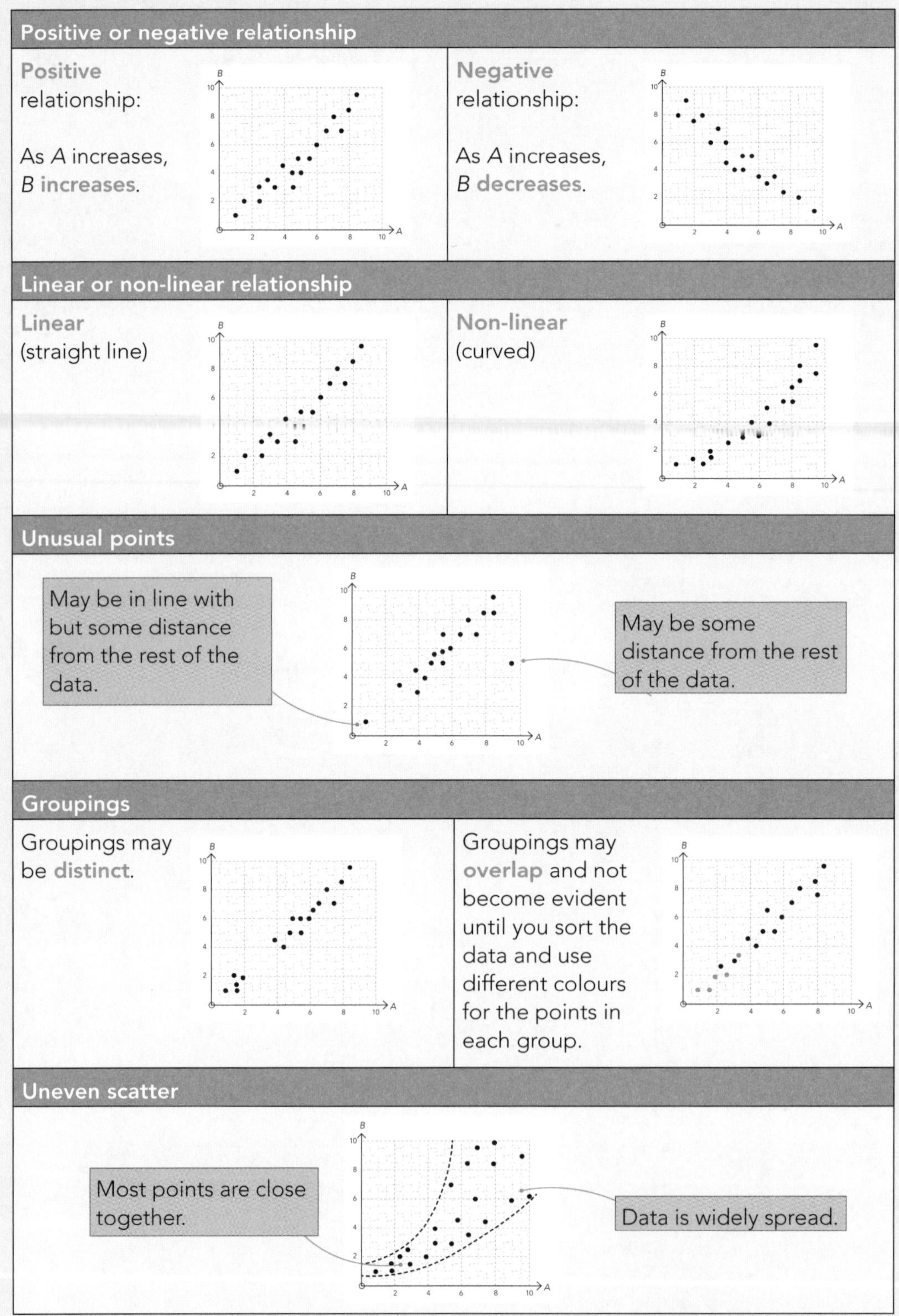

ISBN: 9780170462297

Example: This graph shows the relationship between the age of walkers (years) and the time taken to walk a track (minutes).

*There is a **positive** relationship between the age of walkers and the time it takes to walk a track.*
***This means that** older walkers tended to take longer to walk the track.*
*The relationship appears to be **linear/~~non-linear~~**.*
*There is one **unusual point**: one walker who was 53 years old took only 36 minutes to walk the track. Others of the same age took around an hour.*

Write general descriptions for each of the following sets of data, and identify any features.

1

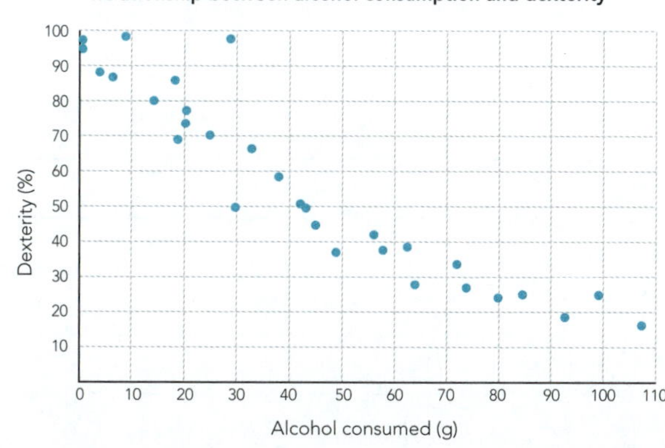

There is a ________________ relationship between ________________________ and ________________________.
This means that as ________________________ increases, ________________________ tends to increase/decrease.
The relationship appears to be linear/non-linear.
Other feature(s): ________________________
____
____

2

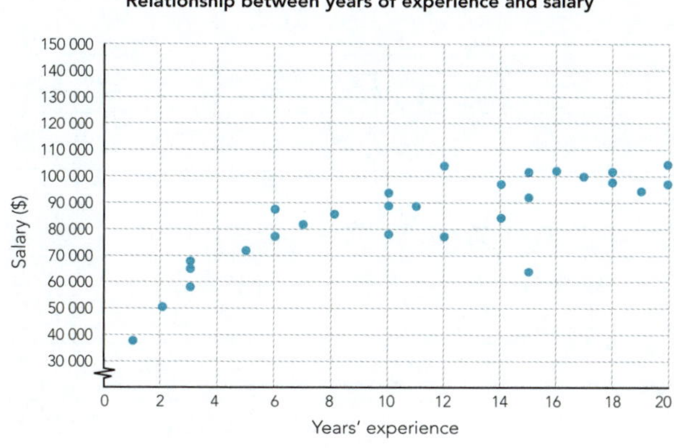

There is a ________________ relationship between ________________________ and ________________________.
This means that as ________________________ increases, ________________________ tends to increase/decrease.
The relationship appears to be linear/non-linear.
Other feature(s): ________________________
____
____

ISBN: 9780170462297

3

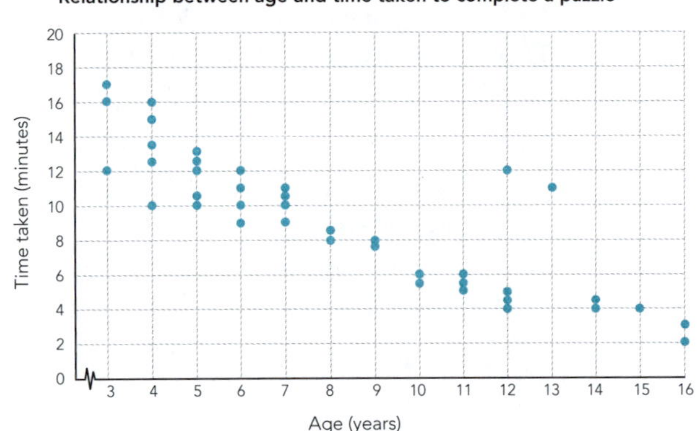

There is a ______________________________

____

____.

This means that as ________________________

____

____.

The relationship appears to be linear/ non-linear.

Other feature(s): __________________________

____

____

4

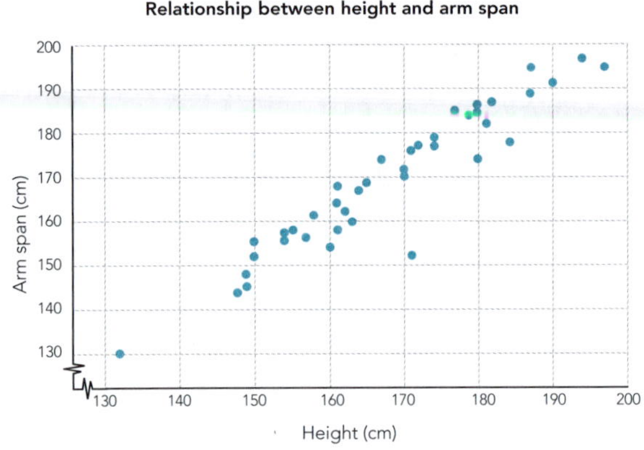

____

____

____

____

____

____

____

____

____

____

5

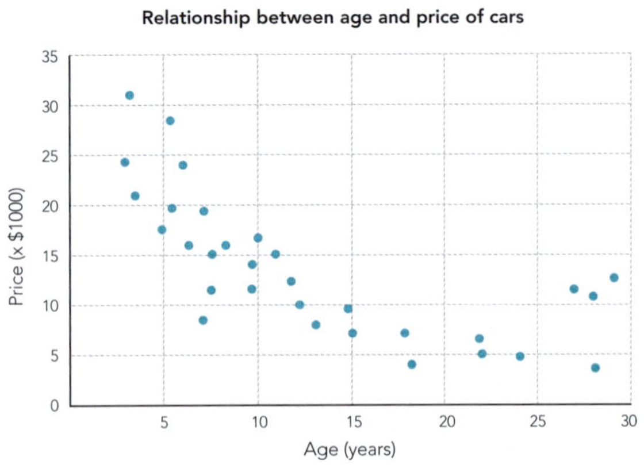

____

____

____

____

____

____

____

____

____

____

 ISBN: 9780170462297

7 Fit a linear model

- To begin with fit a **linear model** to your data.
- This is called a **regression line** or line of best fit.
- Your computer program will calculate the equation for you!

Examples:

1 The graph shows the relationship between the length of the longest fish caught (cm) and the mass of the longest fish caught (kg) by each boat during the Marlborough Sounds fishing competition.

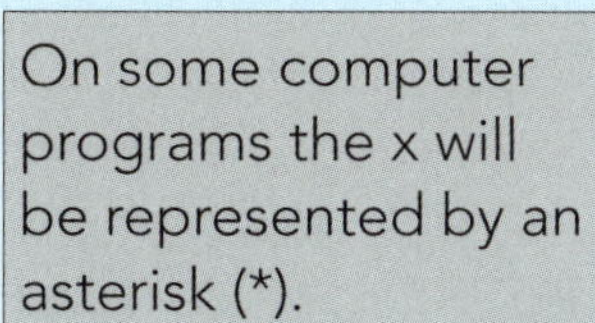

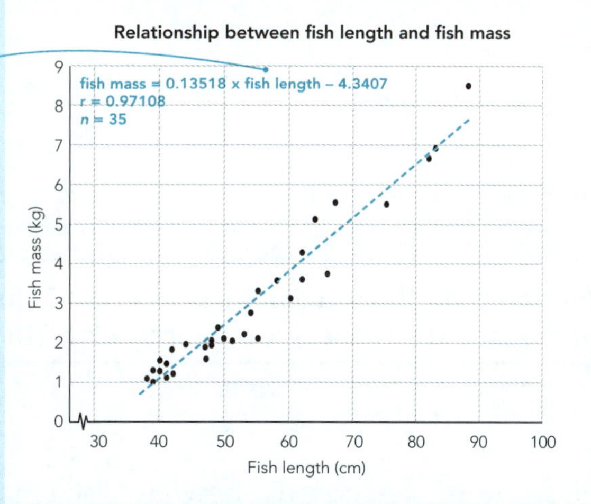

$\therefore$ fish mass (kg) = 0.13518 x fish length (cm) – 4.3407

2 The graph shows the relationship between alcohol (g) consumed and the results of a dexterity test (%) for some Mansfield University students.

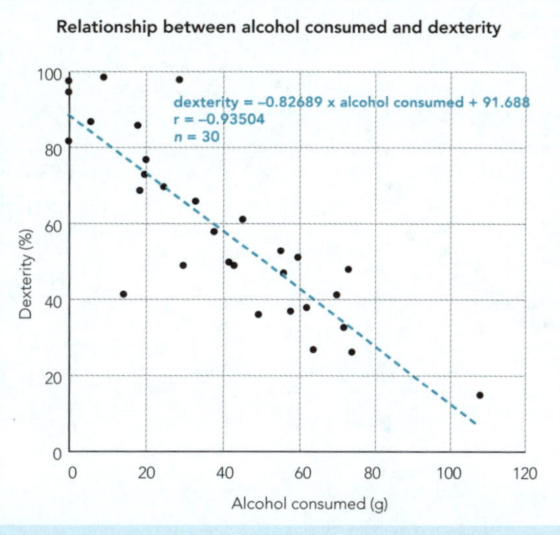

$\therefore$ dexterity (%) = –0.82689 x alcohol consumed (g) + 91.688

Always remember: We are using mathematical models to describe real situations. They will never be perfect.

8 Describe the nature of the relationship

- It is useful to describe the trend of the linear relationship in terms of the **gradient** of the line.
- The nature of the relationship should always be described **in context**.
- The equation of the line is given by the formula $y = mx \pm c$
- The gradient of a line is calculated using the formula

The coefficient of x (m) is the gradient.

$$m = \frac{\text{change in } y}{\text{change in } x} = \frac{\text{rise}}{\text{run}}$$

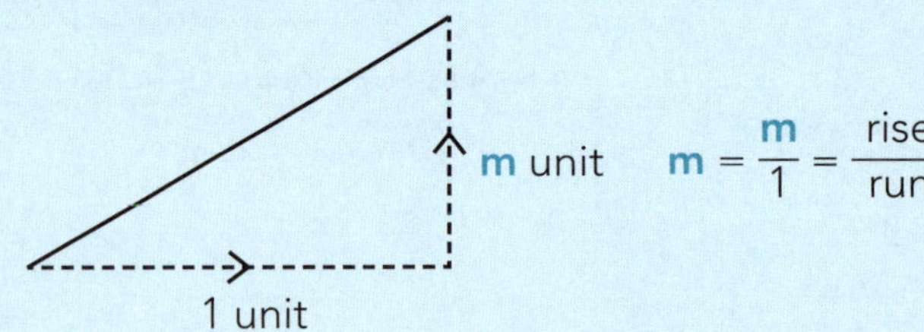

$$m = \frac{m}{1} = \frac{\text{rise}}{\text{run}}$$

As the (variable on the x-axis) increases by 1 (unit), the (the variable on the y-axis) (increases/decreases) on average by (the gradient) (units).

Examples:

1 This graph shows the relationship between fish length and fish mass for the longest fish caught by each boat in the fishing competition.

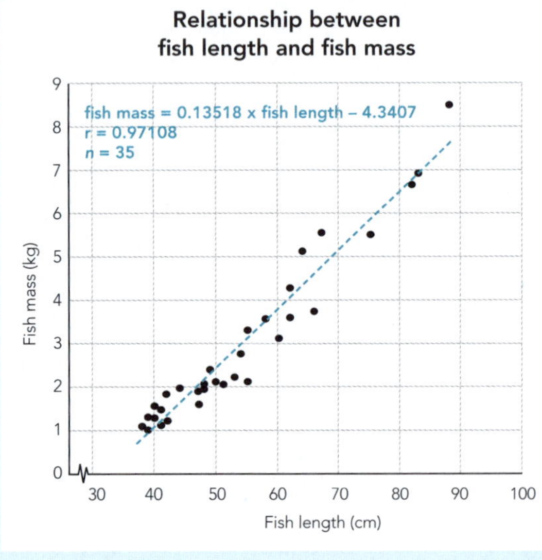

fish mass = **0.13518** x fish length – 4.3407

m = 0.13518

As the **length of the longest fish caught** increases by **1 cm**, we would expect the average **mass of the fish** **increases** on average by **0.13518 kg**.

Positive gradient ⇒ 'increases'

 ISBN: 9780170462297

2 This graph shows the relationship between the age of a child and the time taken to complete a puzzle.

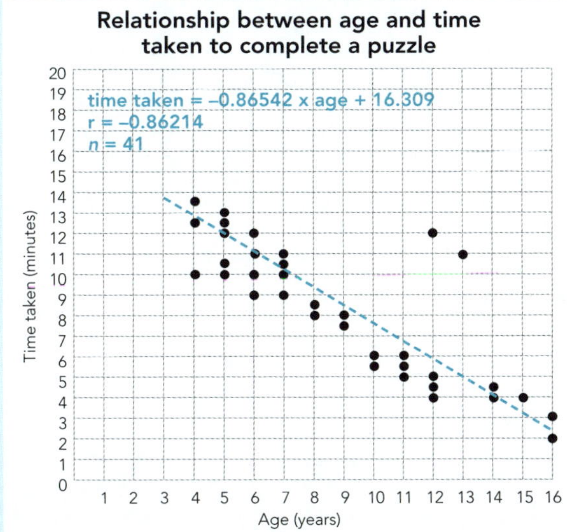

time taken = **–0.86542** x age + 16.309

m = –0.86542

As the **age of a child** increases by **1 year**, we would expect the **time taken to complete the puzzle decreases** on average by **0.86542 minutes.**

Negative gradient ⇒ 'decreases'

Note: Occasionally the units on the *x*-axis might be extremely small, and therefore the gradient is also a very small number. When this happens, multiply **both** the interval on the *x*-axis and the gradient by **the same** power of 10.

For example, as the length of the longest fish caught increases by 1 cm, the average weight of the fish increases on average by 0.13518 kg.

A 1 cm increase ⇒ 0.13518 kg expected increase in the mass of the fish.

⇓ **x 10** ⇓ **x 10**

A 10 cm increase ⇒ 1.3518 kg expected increase in the mass of the fish.

ISBN: 9780170462297

Describe the trend for each of the following graphs.

1 Data from the fishing competition:

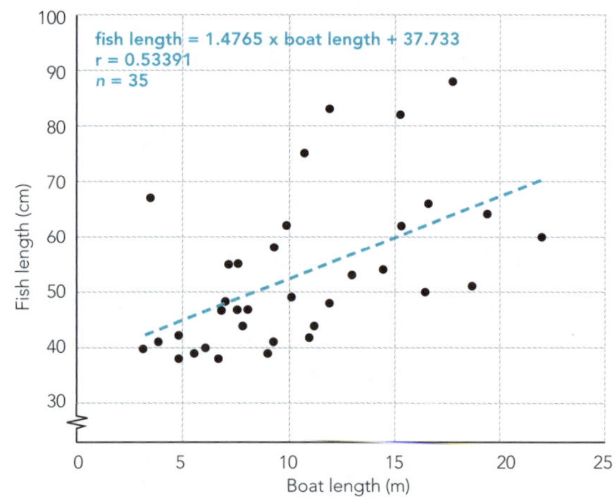

m = ______________

As ______________________________

increases by 1 ________, we would expect

the ______________________________

to increase/decrease on average by

______________________________.

2 Height and arm span were measured for a class of Year 13 students.

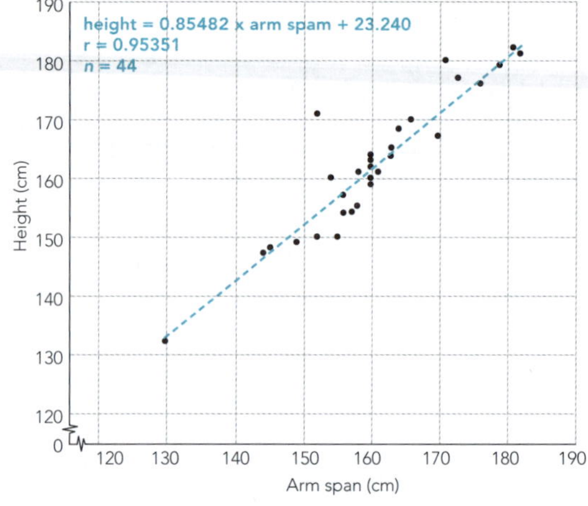

m = ______________

As ______________________________

increases by 1 ________, we would expect

the ______________________________

to increase/decrease on average by

______________________________.

3 The amount of alcohol consumed was recorded for 30 university students, along with their scores in a dexterity test.

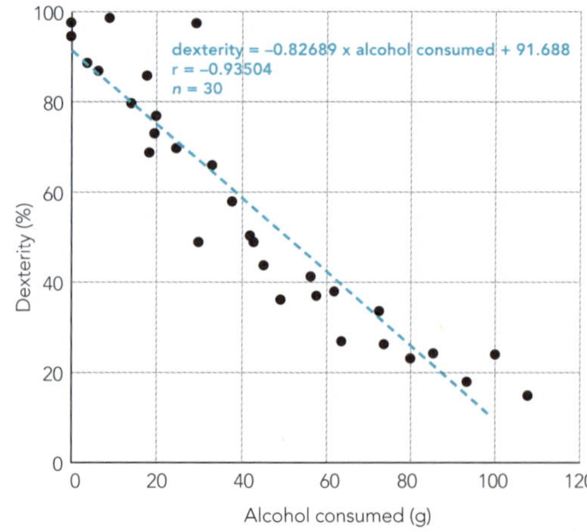

m = ______________

As ______________________________

increases by ________, we would expect

the ______________________________

to increase/decrease on average by

______________________________.

ISBN: 9780170462297

4 Records were kept at a hospital of the birth mass of male babies and their gestational age (weeks since conception).

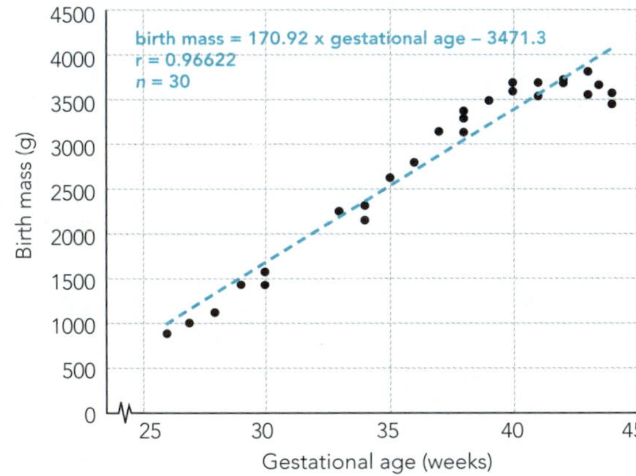

5 The ages and selling prices of second-hand cars were recorded.
Hint: Be careful of the units on the y-axis.

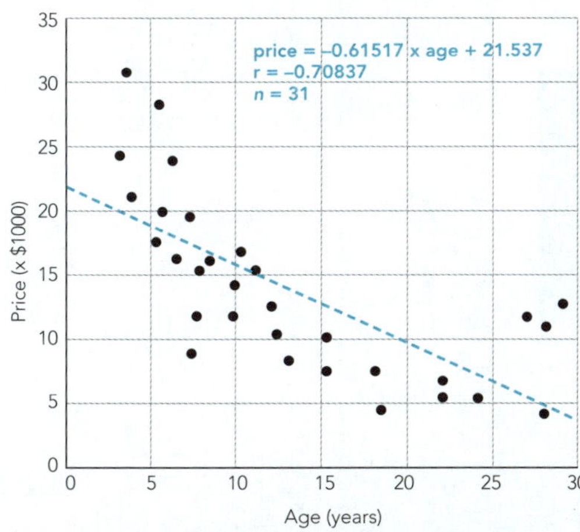

6 Annual salary and the number of years of experience were recorded for 30 IT workers.

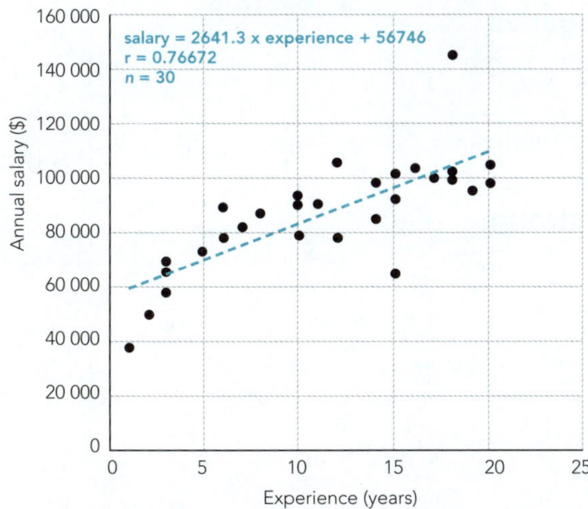

9 Describe the strength of the relationship

The measure for the strength and direction of the relationship is the **correlation coefficient**, **r** (always lower case).

- **r** is a measure of **strength** (of how close the points lie to the line of best fit) and **direction** (whether the relationship is positive or negative).
- It can be used for **straight lines** only.
- Range of values for r: **–1 to +1**.
- The **sign** indicates **direction**:

  +ve ⇒ positive relationship; as x gets bigger, y gets bigger

  –ve ⇒ negative relationship; as x gets bigger, y gets smaller
- The **magnitude** indicates **closeness** of points to the straight line:

  –1 ⇒ perfect negative relationship

  0 ⇒ no relationship

  1 ⇒ perfect positive relationship
- If a **linear** model is fitted, r describes the strength:

$r \geq 0.9$	⇒	very strong
$0.7 \leq r < 0.9$	⇒	strong
$0.5 \leq r < 0.7$	⇒	moderately strong
$0.3 \leq r < 0.5$	⇒	moderately weak
$r < 0.3$	⇒	weak

Example:

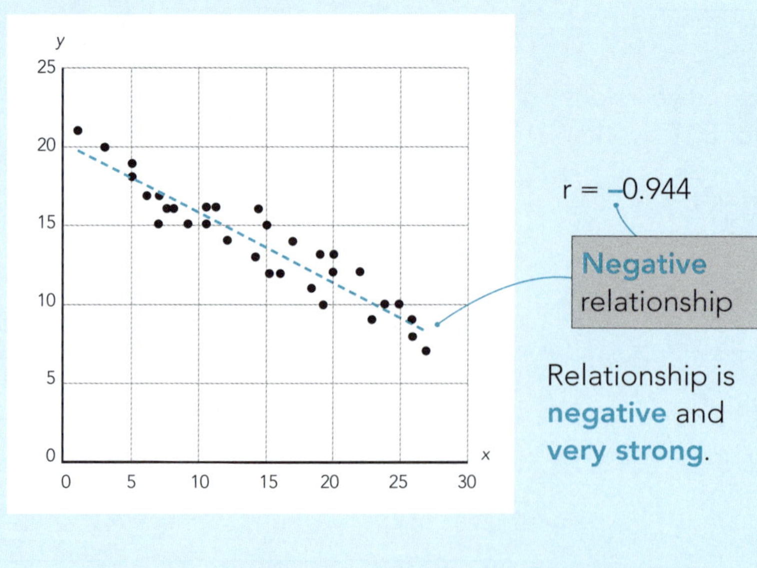

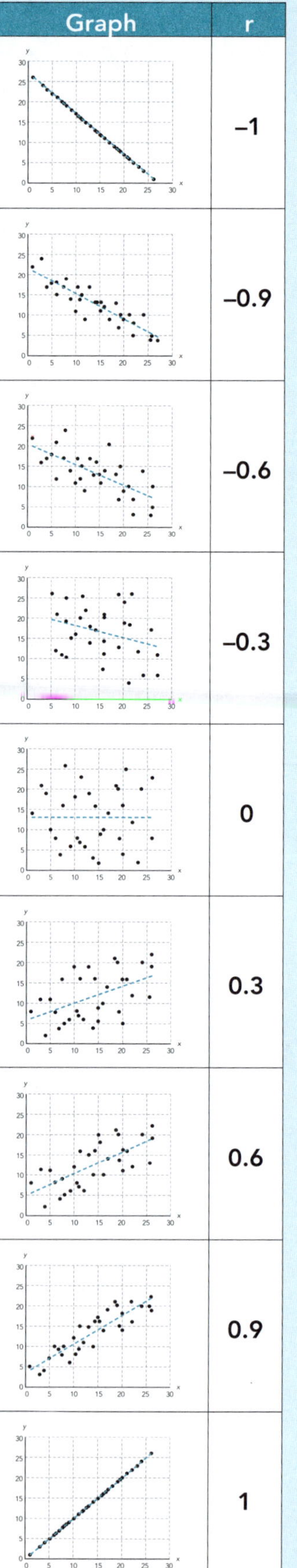

Graph	r
	–1
	–0.9
	–0.6
	–0.3
	0
	0.3
	0.6
	0.9
	1

 ISBN: 9780170462297

Examples:

1

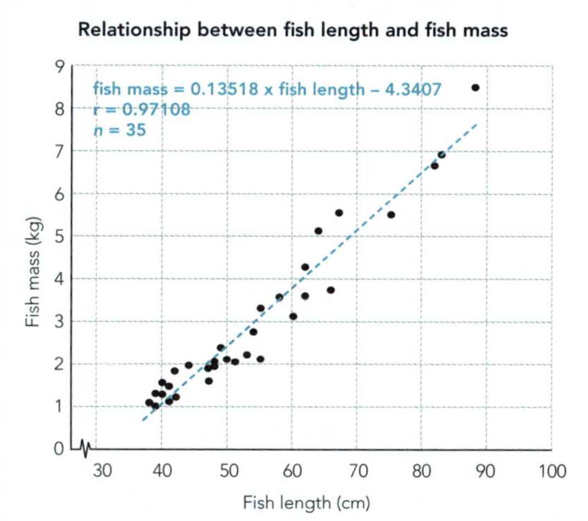

r = 0.97108

Points you should make:

- There is a very strong linear relationship between fish length and fish mass.
- The relationship is very strong because all points are close to the line of best fit, and r is very close to 1.

2

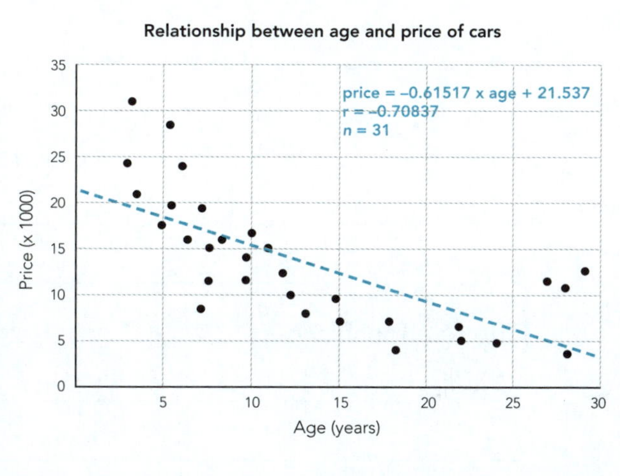

r = –0.70837

Points you should make:

- While the r value would suggest a strong relationship, visually a non-linear trendline may be a better fit.
- The relationship is strong because a number of points are close to the line of best fit, and r is fairly close to –1.

ISBN: 9780170462297

Write down the values of r, and describe the strength of the relationship.

1 Data from the fishing competition:

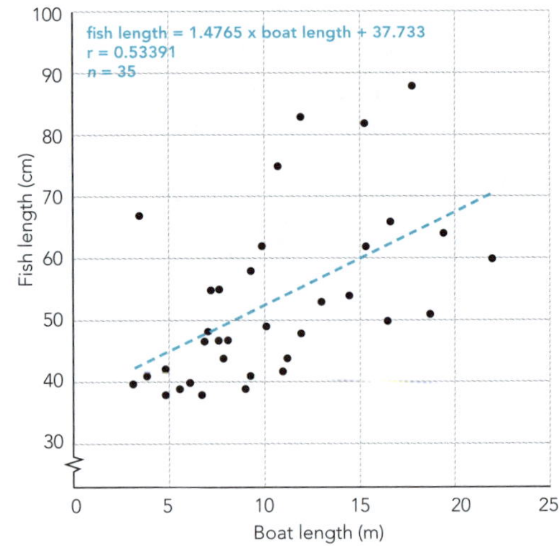

r = ____________________

There is a ____________________________ relationship

between ____

and ____.

The relationship is __________________________________

because ____

____

and r is ____.

2 Arm span and height were measured for a class of Year 13 students.

Relationship between arm span and height for Year 13 students

height = 0.85482 x arm span + 23.240
r = 0.95351
n = 44

Height (cm)

Arm span (cm)

r = ____________________

There is a ____________________________ relationship

between ____

and ____.

The relationship is __________________________________

because ____

____

and r is ____.

ISBN: 9780170462297

3 The age and time taken to complete a puzzle were recorded.

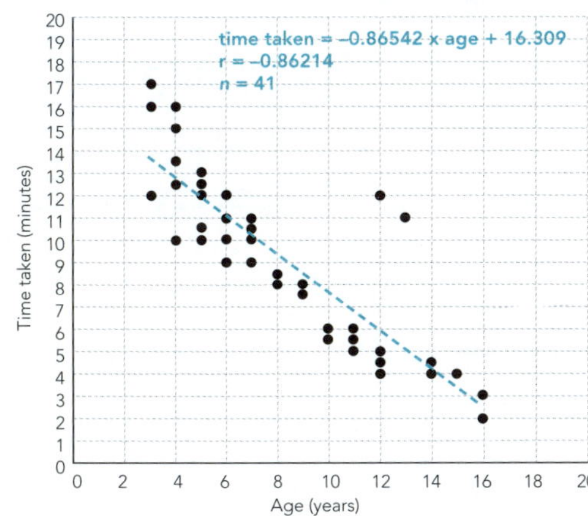

r = ______________

There is a ____

____.

The relationship is ____

____

____

____

____

____.

4 Records were kept at a hospital of the birth mass of male babies and their gestational age (weeks since conception).

Relationship between gestational age and birth mass

birth mass = 170.92 x gestational age − 3471.3
r = 0.96622
n = 30

Birth mass (g)

Gestational age (weeks)

r = ______________

There is a ____

____.

The relationship is ____

____

____

____

____

____.

ISBN: 9780170462297

5 The amount of alcohol consumed was recorded for 30 adults, along with their scores in a dexterity test.

r = ______

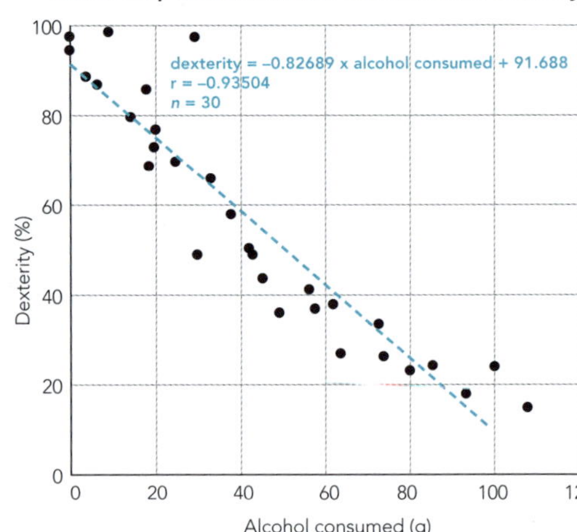

6 Annual salary and the number of years of experience were recorded for 30 IT workers.

r = ______

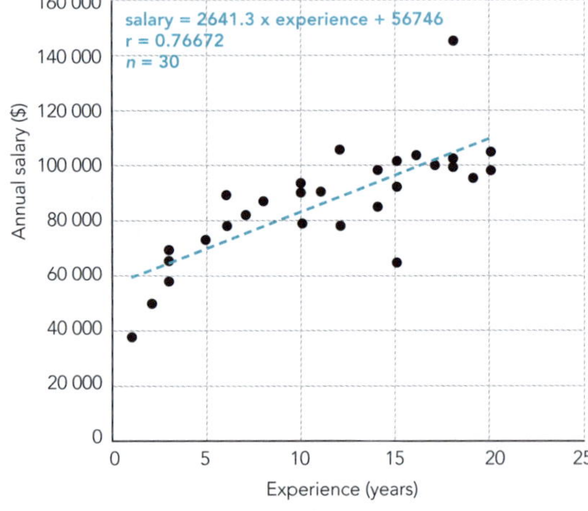

 ISBN: 9780170462297

10 Use the model to make a prediction

- Because we are using mathematical models to describe real situations, we can never be certain that predictions will be accurate. Therefore they should be rounded appropriately.
- How accurate they are will depend on:
  — how well the model fits the data
  — the type of prediction being made.

There are two types of prediction that you should make: interpolation and extrapolation.

Interpolation — where a prediction is made within the range of the data.

Examples:

1 Estimate the mass of a 70 cm fish.

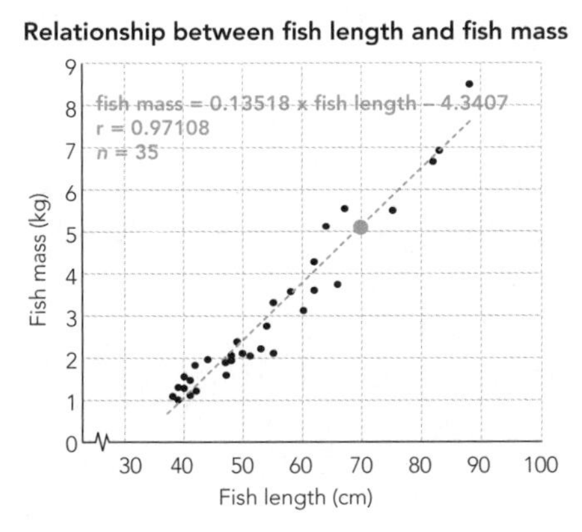

From the graph, we would estimate that the mass of a 70 cm fish would be about 5.2 kg.

From the equation, we can calculate a more accurate estimate:

fish mass = 0.13518 x 70 – 4.3407
= 5.1219 kg
Round to 5.1 kg

Check that this is similar to your estimate from the graph.

Observations: 1 The relationship is very strong.
2 We are estimating within the range of the data.

As a result: We would expect this estimate to be reasonably accurate.

2 Estimate the length of a fish caught on a 14 m boat.

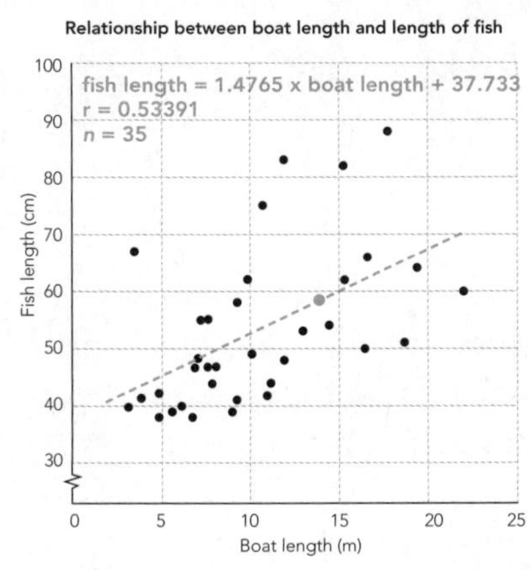

From the graph, we would estimate that the length of a fish caught by a 14 m boat would be just under 60 cm.

From the equation, we can calculate a more accurate estimate:

fish length = 1.4765 x 14 + 37.733
= 58.404 cm
Round to 58.4 cm

Observations: 1 The relationship is moderately strong.
2 We are estimating within the range of the data.

As a result: Although we are estimating within the range of the data, the relationship is moderately weak, so we could not have great confidence in this prediction.

Extrapolation — where a prediction is made **beyond** the range of the data.

Examples:

1 Estimate the length of a fish caught on a 23 m boat.

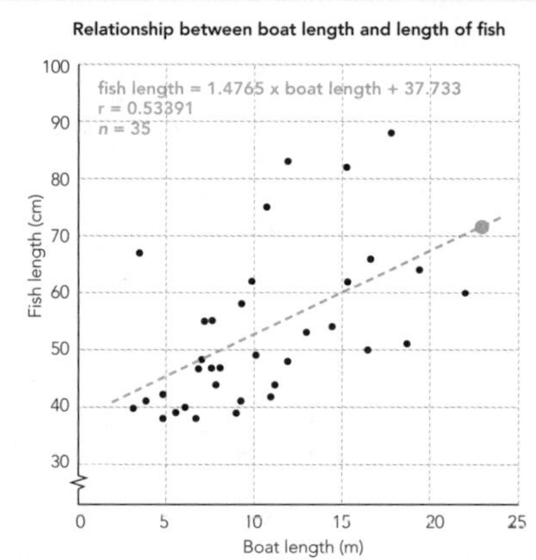

From the **graph**, we would estimate that the length of a fish caught by a 23 m boat would be around 70 cm.

From the **equation**, we can calculate a more accurate estimate:

fish length = 1.4765 x 23 + 37.733
= 71.6925 cm
Round to 71.7 cm

Observations:
1. The relationship is moderately strong.
2. We are estimating beyond the range of the data. We have assumed that the linear model continues beyond the boat length of 22 m, but this may not be the case.

As a result: We would **not** expect this estimate to be very accurate.

2 Estimate the mass of a 100 cm fish.

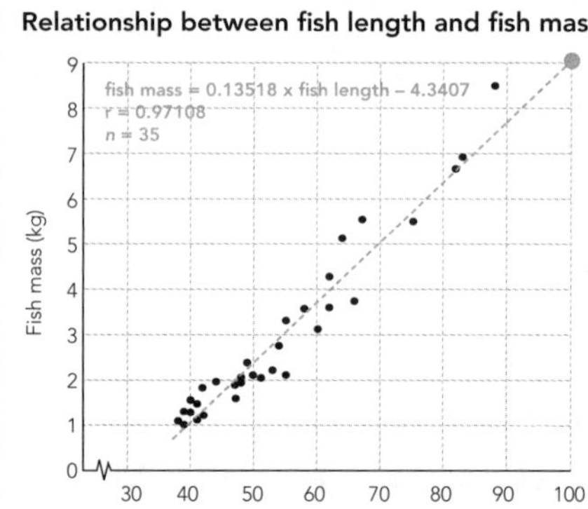

From the **graph**, we would estimate that the mass of a 100 cm fish would be about 9 kg.

From the **equation**, we can calculate a more accurate estimate:

fish mass = 0.13518 x 100 – 4.3407
= 9.1773 kg
Round to 9.2 kg

Observations:
1. The relationship is very strong.
2. We are estimating well beyond the range of the data, and we have assumed that the linear model continues beyond a fish length of 88 cm. However, this may not be the case, particularly because there is very little data for fish that are longer than 70 cm.

As a result: Although the relationship is very strong, we cannot have great confidence in this prediction. A prediction for 90 cm would probably be more reliable because it is closer to the data.

Warning: Extrapolating a long way beyond the data is not recommended and likely to be inaccurate.

ISBN: 9780170462297

Make the predictions required in each question, and comment on the accuracy of each.

1 Estimate the mass of the longest fish caught by a 12 m boat during the fishing competition.

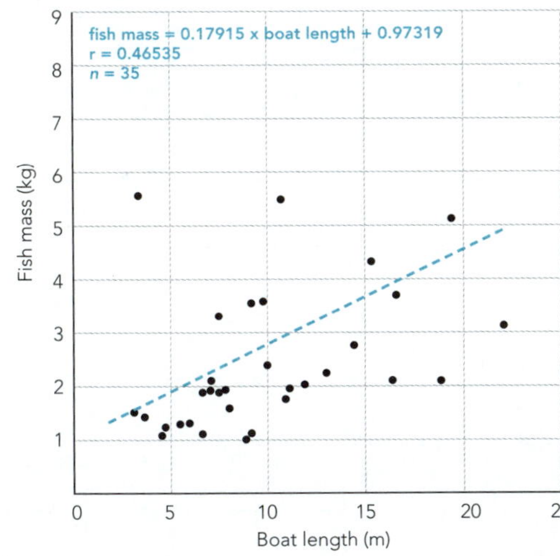

Interpolation/Extrapolation?

Estimate: Mass ≈ 3 kg

Calculation: Mass = 0.17915 x 12 + 0.97319

= 3.12299 kg

Observations:

1 The relationship is ______________.

2 We are estimating *within/beyond* the range of the data.

As a result: ______________

____

____

____

____

____

____

2 Estimate the height of a Year 13 student with a 190 cm arm span.

Relationship between arm span and height for Year 13 students

height = 0.85482 x arm span + 23.240
r = 0.95351
n = 44

Height (cm)

Arm span (cm)

Interpolation/Extrapolation?

Estimate: Height ≈ ______________

Calculation: Height = ______________

= ______________

Observations:

1 The relationship is ______________.

2 We are estimating *within/beyond* the range of the data.

As a result: ______________

____

____

____

____

____

____

ISBN: 9780170462297

3 Estimate the time it would take an 18-year-old to complete the puzzle.

Relationship between age and time taken to complete a puzzle

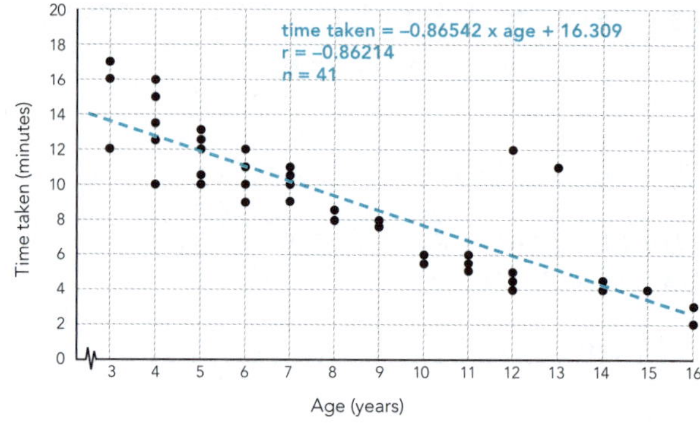

Interpolation/Extrapolation?

Estimate: Time ≈ ______________

Calculation: Time = ______________

= ______________

Observations:

____

____

____

____

____

As a result: ____

____

____

____

____

4 Estimate the mass of a male baby that is born at a gestational age of 32 weeks.

Relationship between gestational age and birth mass

birth mass = 170.92 x gestational age − 3471.3
r = 0.96622
n = 30

Birth mass (g)

Gestational age (weeks)

Interpolation/Extrapolation?

Estimate: Birth mass ≈ ______________

Calculation: Birth mass = ______________

= ______________

Observations:

____

____

____

____

____

As a result: ____

____

____

____

____

ISBN: 9780170462297

5 Estimate the score in the dexterity test for an adult who had consumed 90 g of alcohol.

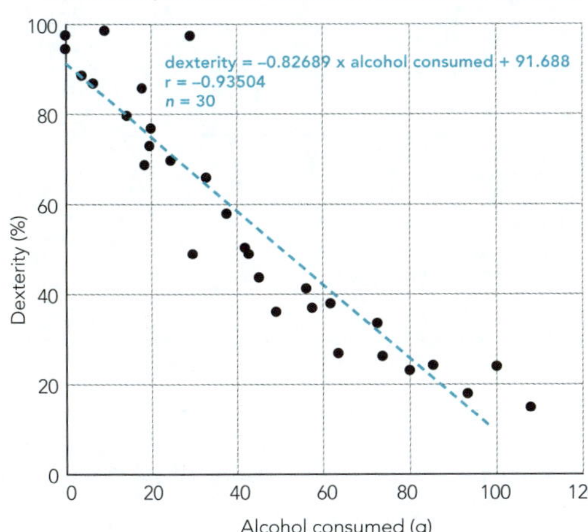

6 Estimate the salary of an IT worker who has 23 years' experience.

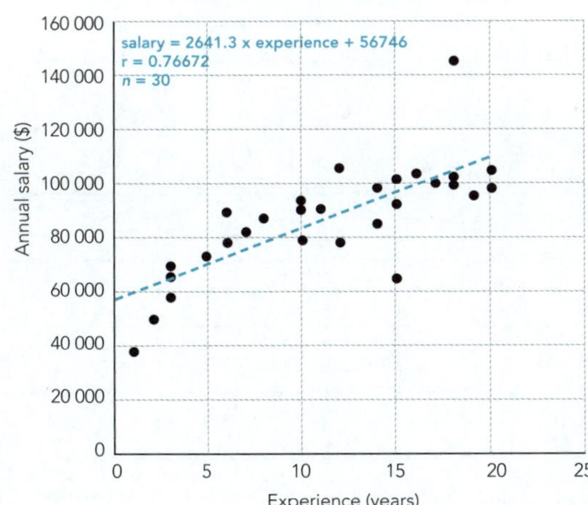

ISBN: 9780170462297

Make some predictions of your own, and discuss them with your neighbour or teacher.

7

8

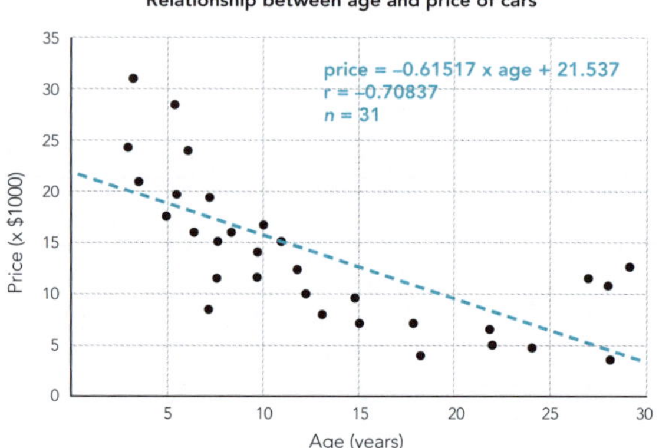

ISBN: 9780170462297

11 Communicate findings in a conclusion

In your conclusion you should:
- Answer your question.
- Repeat earlier important points.
- Make a judgement as to which model (trend line) is the most useful and why.
- Discuss whether the information you have learnt in your report is useful and whether it fulfils your purpose.
- Discuss limitations of the study and suggest ways in which it could be improved.
- **Not** include new information. This is where you should be summing up your ideas and coming to your final point.

Putting it all together

The following are the requirements for a basic report. These have been numbered in the report on pages 40–41.

1. Research your context, and then select suitable data.
2. Pose an appropriate question which is informed by contextual knowledge.
3. Identify and fully describe the response variable and the explanatory variable, with the units involved. Justify your choice.
4. State the purpose of your investigation and who would find it useful.
5. Plot the data. You **must** put the explanatory variable on the x-axis and the response variable on the y-axis.
6. Identify features in the data, i.e. positive or negative, linear or not, unusual points or groupings.
7. Fit a linear trend line, including the equation.
8. Describe the nature of the relationship, ideally using the gradient of the line.
9. Describe and justify the strength of the relationship.
10. Make at least one prediction. Include units and link them to the context.
11. Write a conclusion. Make sure it answers your question and link it to the purpose of your report.

ISBN: 9780170462297

Bivariate basic report — fishing

Research indicates that fishing competitions have different rules and regulations and there isn't a New Zealand-wide 'standard' set of requirements. A number of fishing competitions seem to require the length of the fish to be measured with a specific measuring device. A photo can then be taken as proof of the catch (https://www.fishingcomp.co.nz/rules/). Other competitions require competitors to bring their catch to a weigh station to be judged (https://www.westhaven.co.nz/westhaven/news-events/auckland-fishing-classic-competition-rules/). A competition based on length allows for catch and release whereas weigh-ins would result in the death of the fish. Some competitions also have boat (e.g. kayak) and fisher people categories (e.g. junior).

1 Research context.

Is there a relationship between the length of the longest fish (cm) and the mass of the longest fish caught (kg), and if so, what its nature?
The data in this report has been obtained from a fishing competition in the Marlborough Sounds.

2 Appropriate question.

I have chosen fish length to be the explanatory variable and fish weight to be the response variable. I think that the mass of the fish can, in part, be explained by its length. Measuring the length of a fish on 'official' measuring devices may help fisher people estimate the mass of their catch. This report may be useful to those entering a competition which is judged by weight rather than length. It could enable them to estimate the mass of the fish from the length before getting it officially measured at the weigh-in.

3 Explanatory and response variables identified.

4 Purpose.

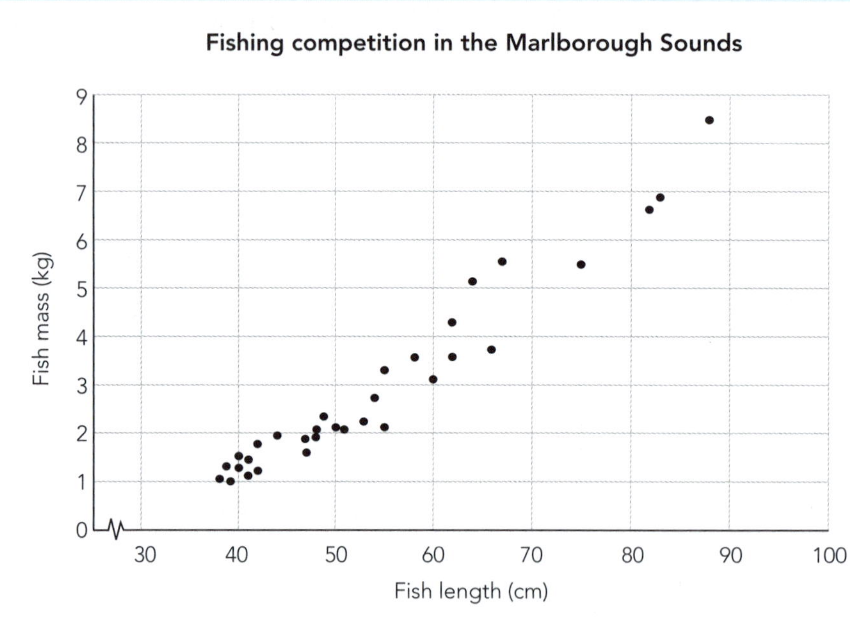

5 Graph with explanatory variable on x-axis.

From the graph, it can be seen that the data is distributed from bottom left to top right. This indicates a positive relationship between fish length and fish mass, and suggests that as the fish length increases, the fish mass tends to increase. The distribution of data also indicates that a linear regression line could be suitable.

6 Identify features.

ISBN: 9780170462297

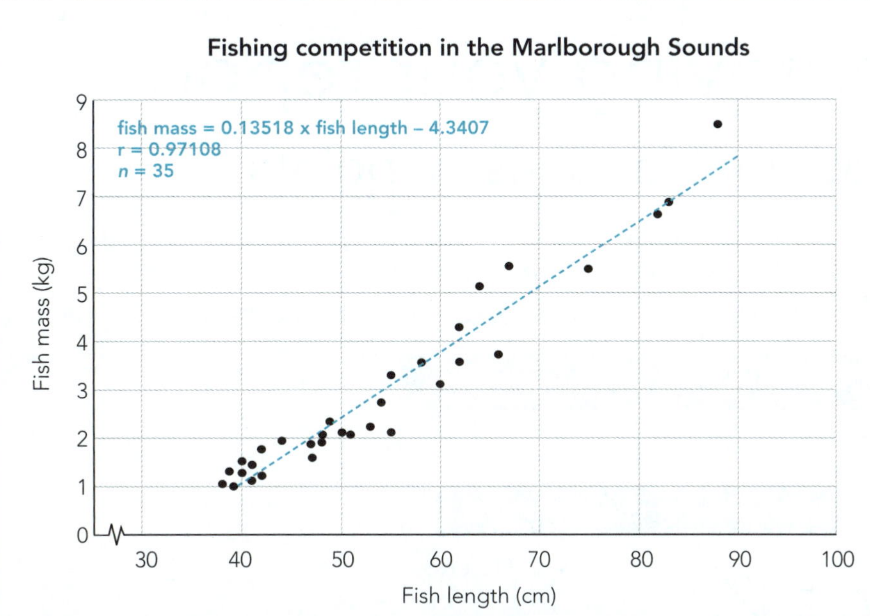

7 Fit a linear trend line.

As mentioned earlier, as the fish length increases, its mass tends to increase. More specifically, as the length of the longest fish caught increases by 1 cm, the average mass of the fish increases by 0.13518 kg.

8 Describe the nature with gradient.

There appears to be a strong relationship between fish length and fish mass. I think the relationship is strong because the data points are reasonably close to the regression line and the r value is 0.97108, which is very close to 1.

9 Describe and justify strength.

There is one unusual feature: a large fish that has a length of 88 cm and a mass of 8.51 kg. Not only is it larger than any of the other fish, but it is also a bit further above the trend line than expected.

I have fitted a linear regression line on the graph and the equation is:

fish mass (kg) = 0.13518 x fish length (cm) – 4.3407

I can use the equation of the regression line to make a prediction. If we caught a fish that was 80 cm long, we would expect it to weigh around 6.47 kg (2 dp). The relationship is strong and we are estimating within the range of the data (interpolation), so we would expect our estimate to be reasonably accurate.

10 Prediction.

In conclusion, there is a strong, positive, linear relationship between the length of the longest fish and the mass of the longest fish. Making a prediction from our regression line could be of use to fisher people in competitions around New Zealand. It could also enable competitions to be judged on photographs of fish on standard measuring devices. This would mean that fish could be released alive after being caught. If further investigation were to be undertaken, I would recommend a larger sample. It could also be interesting to repeat this analysis separately for each of the different species of fish.

11 Conclusion.

ISBN: 9780170462297

Improving your report

A An in-depth look at unusual points

Points can be unusual for two reasons:

1 They are a long way from the line of best fit.
2 They are close to the line of best fit, but some distance from the rest of the data.

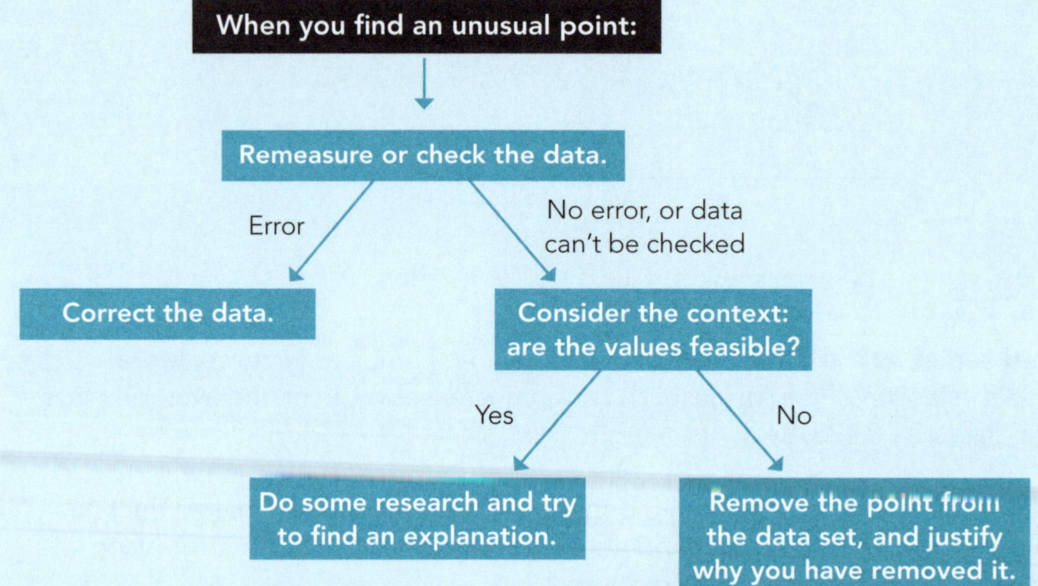

Example:

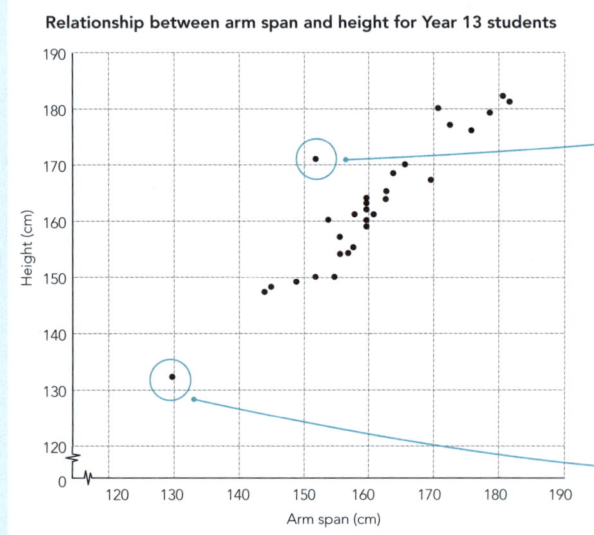

Not in line with the rest of the data, and this person is much taller than we would expect for somebody with an arm span of 152 cm.
Things to find out:

1 If possible, who were they, and check the data.
2 Research the range of ratios between arm span and height to discover whether the values are unreasonable or not.

In line with the rest of the data, but this person is much shorter and has much shorter arms than any other student.
Things to find out:

1 If possible, who were they, and check the data. Was this a very young Year 13 student?
2 Would these values be reasonable for an achondroplastic person (dwarf)?

Not all data includes unusual points. Do not say that points are unusual unless they really are.

ISBN: 9780170462297

Decide whether there are unusual points in the following graphs, write down their approximate coordinates, say why you think they are unusual, and what you would need to research.

Note:

1 Normally you will have the actual data, so you can give *exact* values for unusual points.

2 In your report, you will need to do the research, and quote your references.

1

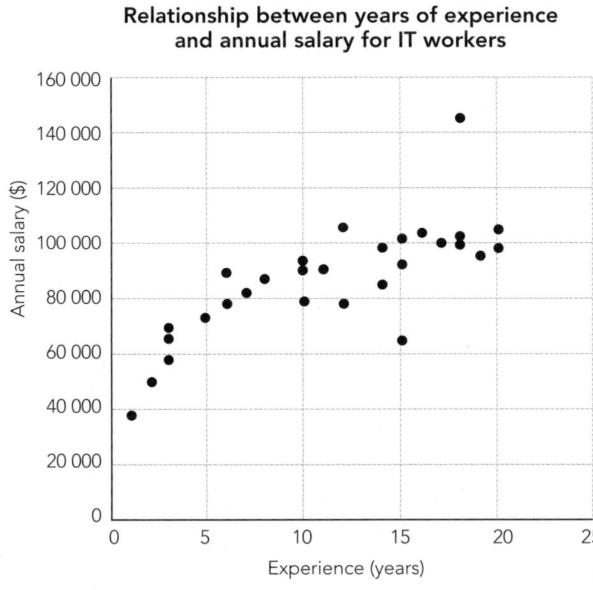

2

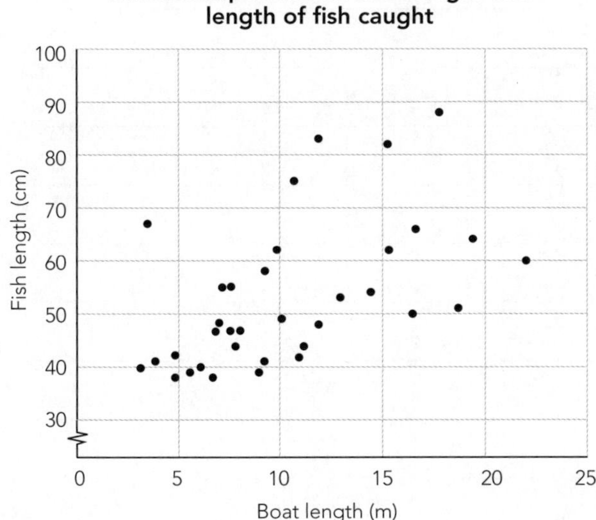

ISBN: 9780170462297

3

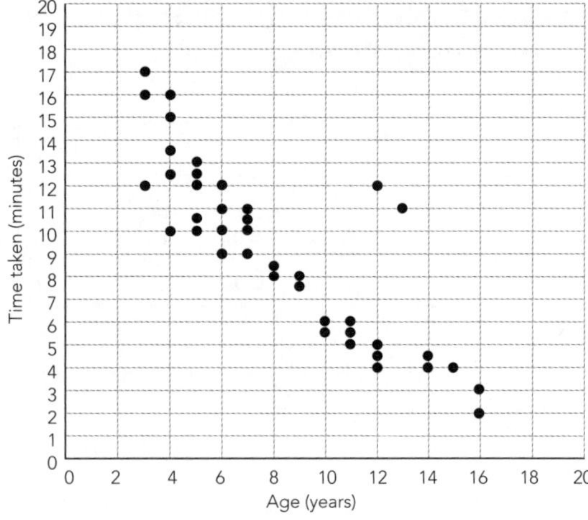

4

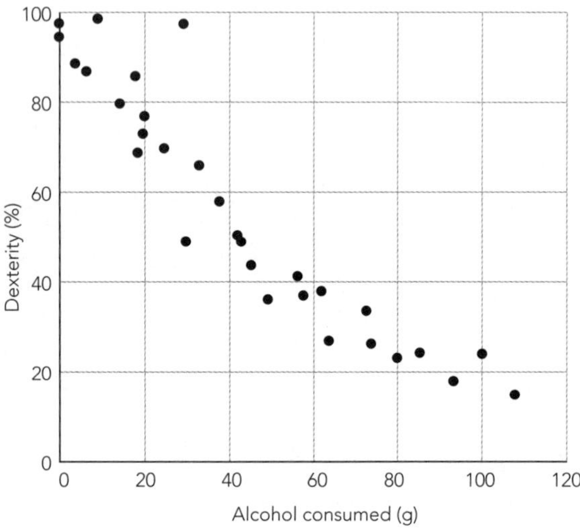

ISBN: 9780170462297

B By removing unusual points

- Do **not** remove unusual points from the data without **discussion** and **justification**.
- Your **first** analysis of the data should always **include** the unusual point.
- Then **re-analyse** the data without the unusual point.
- Discuss the **differences** between the two analyses.
- Redo your **predictions** using the improved model.

Example:

Relationship including the unusual points:

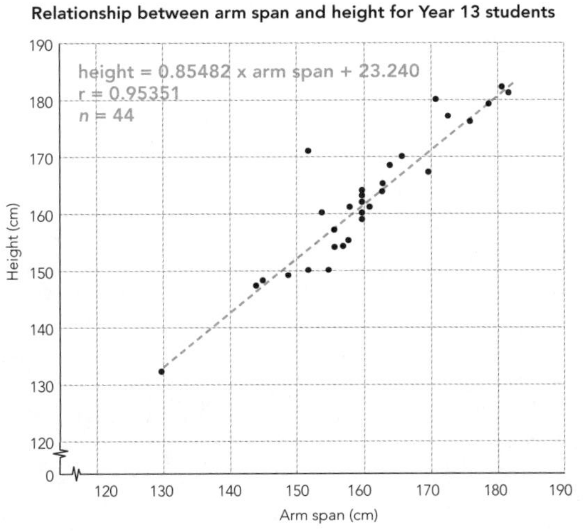

I will re-analyse this data without the points (130, 132) and (152, 171). I will do this because I believe that it is very unusual for a Year 13 student to be just 132 cm high. I think that it is also very unusual for a person who is 171 cm high to have an arm span of just 152 cm. One of the measurements may not have been made correctly, or else this represents a person with extremely short arms in relation to their height.

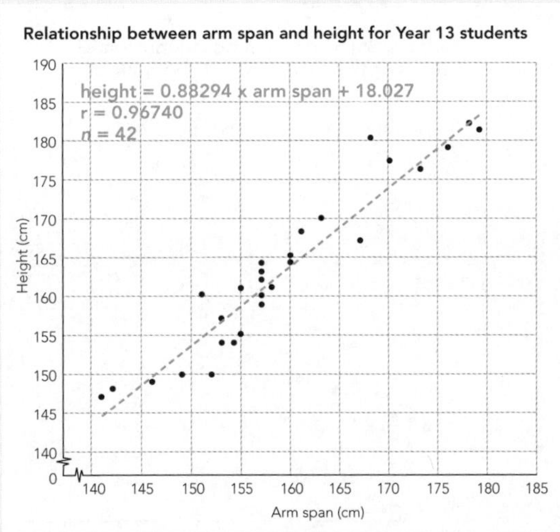

Removing the unusual points means:

1 The slope of the line of best fit changes from 0.85482 to 0.88294. This means we would expect that for Year 13 students, an increase of 1 cm in length in arm span would result in a slightly bigger (0.88 cm) increase in height. This compares with an increase of 0.85 cm when the unusual points were included.

2 The r value increases from 0.95351 to 0.96740. This means that the data without the unusual points, on average, lies slightly closer to the line of best fit.

ISBN: 9780170462297

Discuss the difference made by the removal of the unusual points.

1

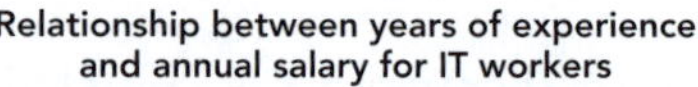

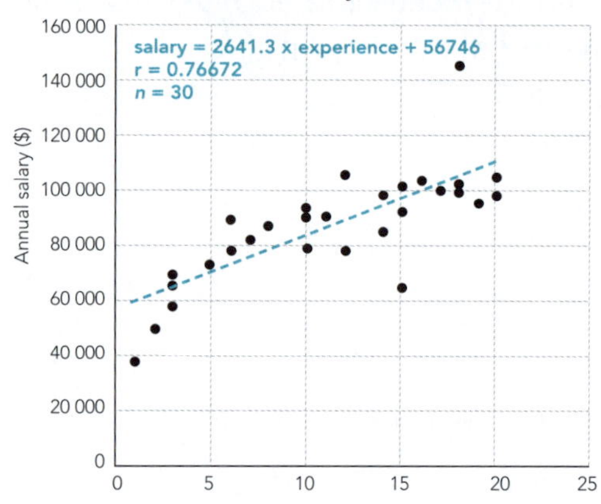

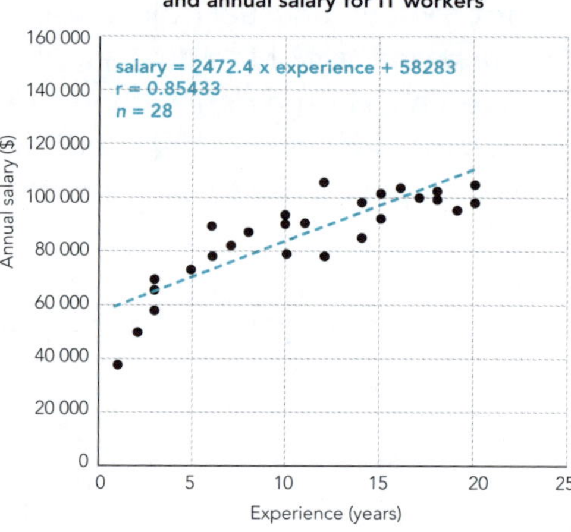

The slope of the line of best fit changes from ____________ to ____________.

This means that ____

____

____

The r value increases from ____________ to ____________.

This means that ____

____

____

2

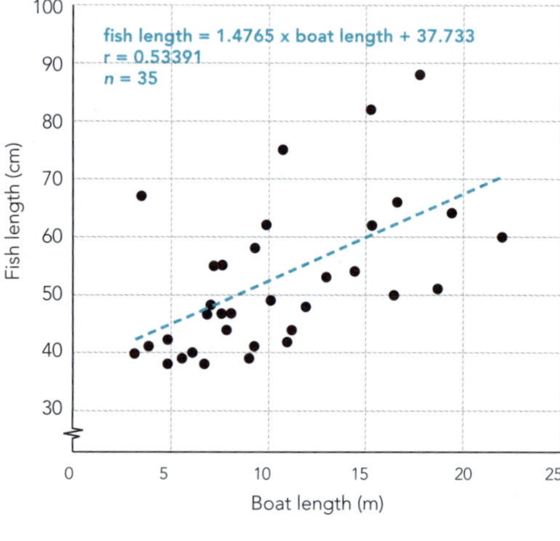

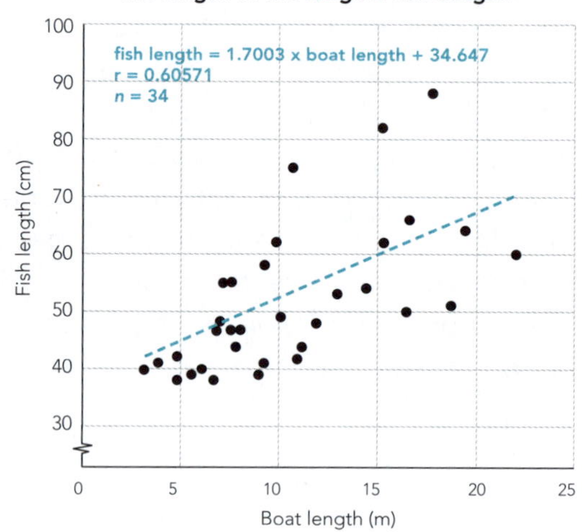

____

____

____

____

____

ISBN: 9780170462297

C Analyse the residual graph

- The residual of a point is the **vertical difference** between the point and line of best fit (regression line).
- **Irregularities** in the distribution of the residuals can suggest that a **curve** may be a closer fit for the data, rather than a straight line.
- The fitted value of the **response** variable is on the **horizontal** axis.
- If the relationship is **positive**, then the locations of the data points are the **same**. If the relationship is **negative**, then the locations of the data points are a mirror image.

How residuals are calculated

The residual for (x, y) = y – (mx + c)

y value of the point

What the *y* value would be if it were on the regression line.

Example: Here is data from the fishing competition:

Residual graph for the same data:

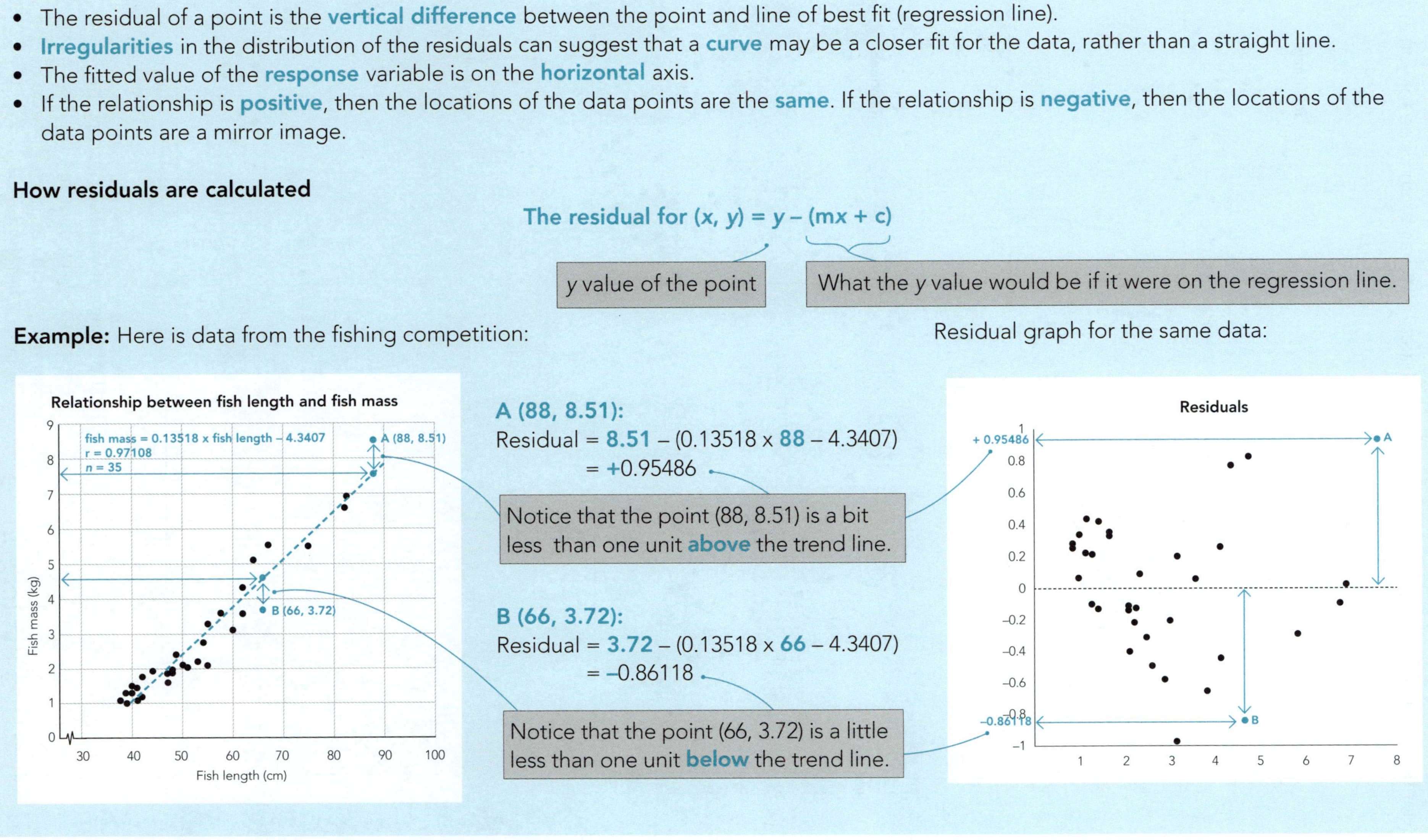

A (88, 8.51):

Residual = **8.51** – (0.13518 x **88** – 4.3407)

= **+0.95486**

Notice that the point (88, 8.51) is a bit less than one unit **above** the trend line.

B (66, 3.72):

Residual = **3.72** – (0.13518 x **66** – 4.3407)

= **–0.86118**

Notice that the point (66, 3.72) is a little less than one unit **below** the trend line.

ISBN: 9780170462297

Identify points A, B, C and D on these residual graphs (A has been done for you in questions **1** and **3**).

1

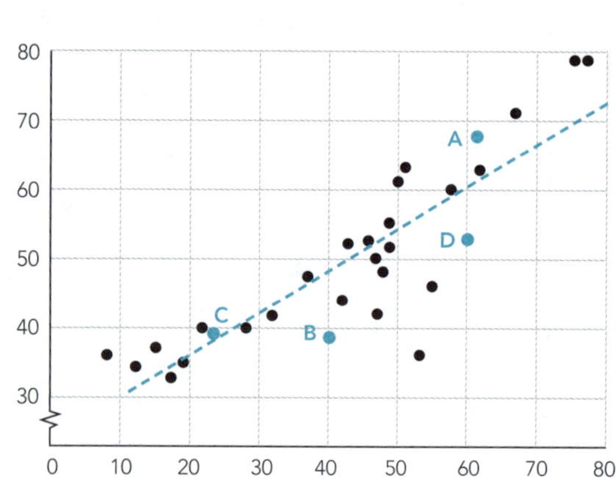

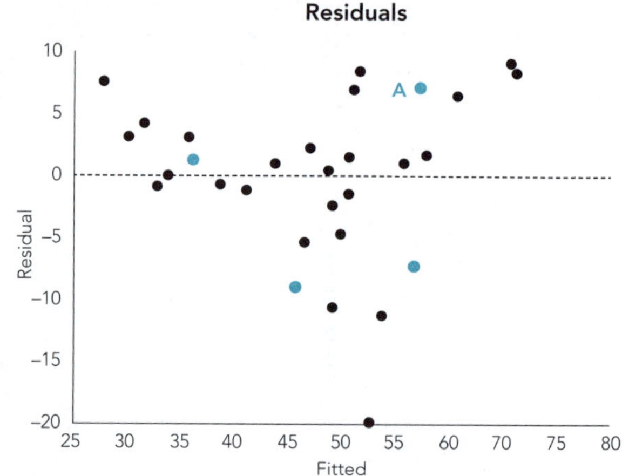

2

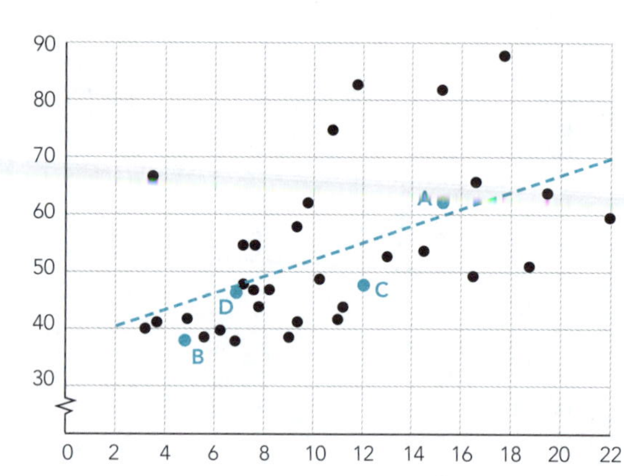

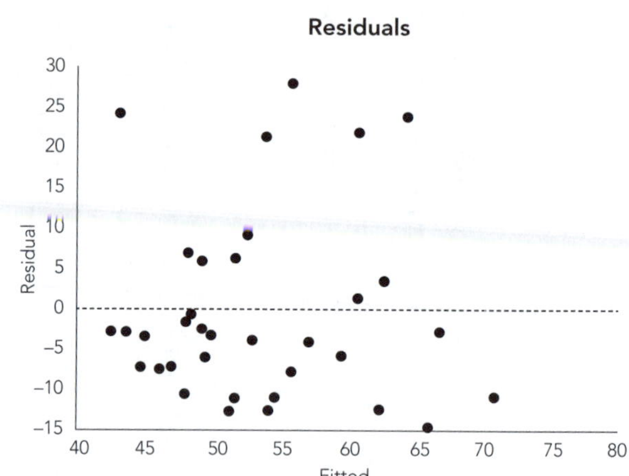

3

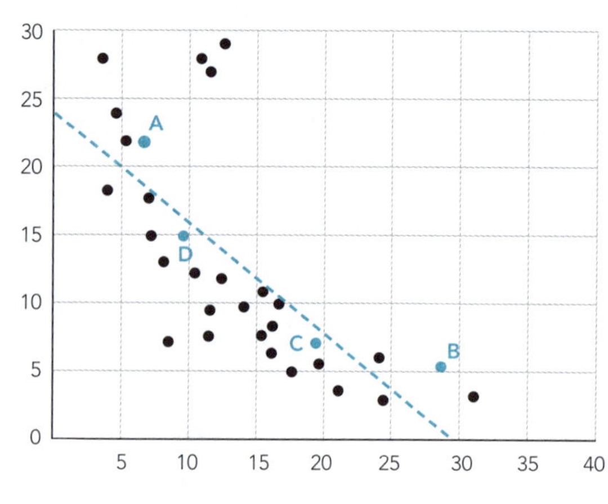

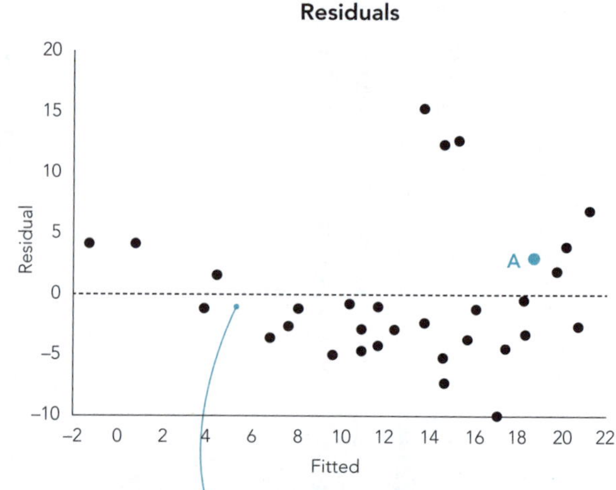

For a negative relationship: the response (y) values are on this axis, so this graph is a mirror image of what you might expect.

 ISBN: 9780170462297

Interpreting residuals

1 Where a straight line is the best regression line for the data

Notice that there is an **even** distribution of points above and below this regression line.

Consequently, the residuals are **evenly spread** above and below the horizontal axis.

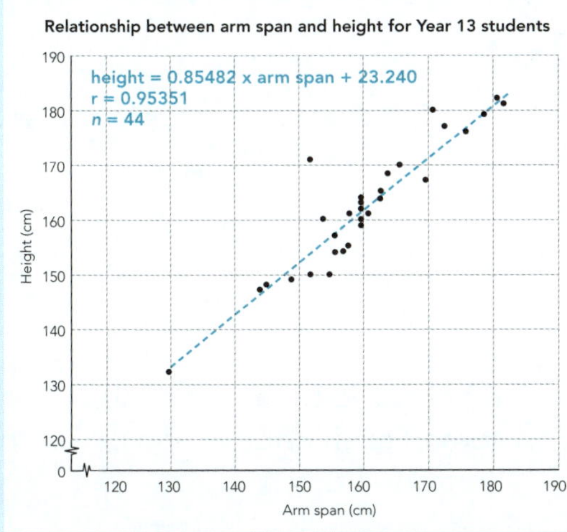

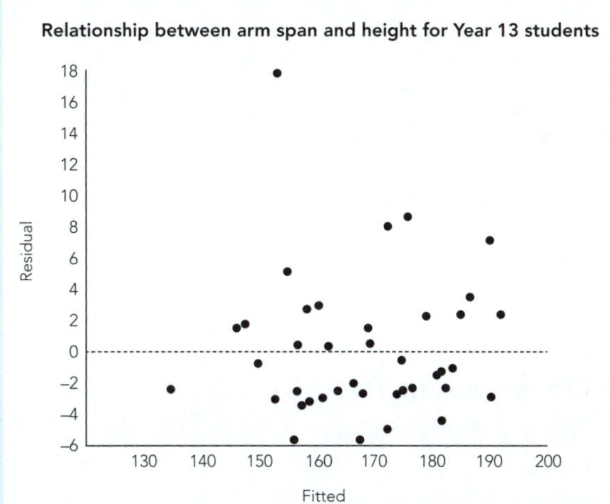

Conclusion: The residuals are fairly evenly spread from about –6 to 6, above and below the horizontal axis, which suggests a straight regression line will be the best for this data.

2 Where a curve is the best regression line for the data

Notice that there is an **uneven** distribution of points above and below this regression line.

Consequently, the residuals are **unevenly spread** above and below the horizontal axis.

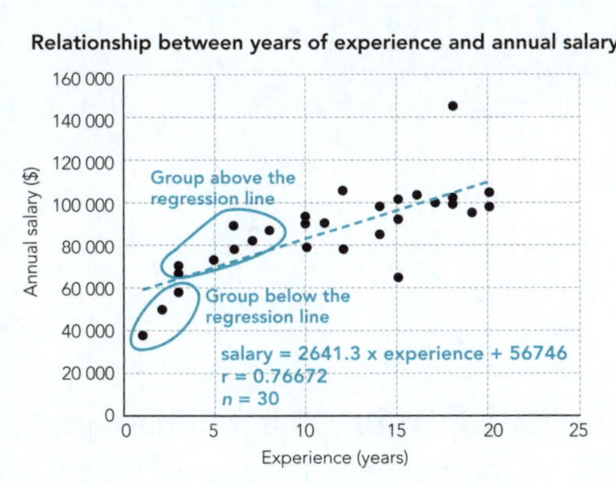

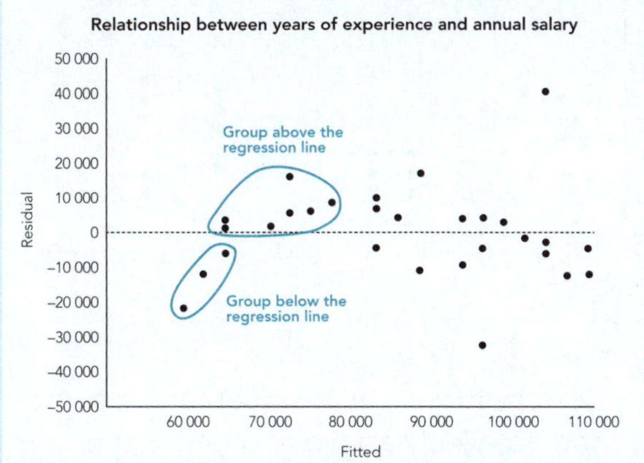

Conclusion: The residuals are not spread evenly above and below the horizontal axis, so a curve is likely to be a best fit for this data.

ISBN: 9780170462297

Identify what you observe and what you can conclude about these residual graphs.

1

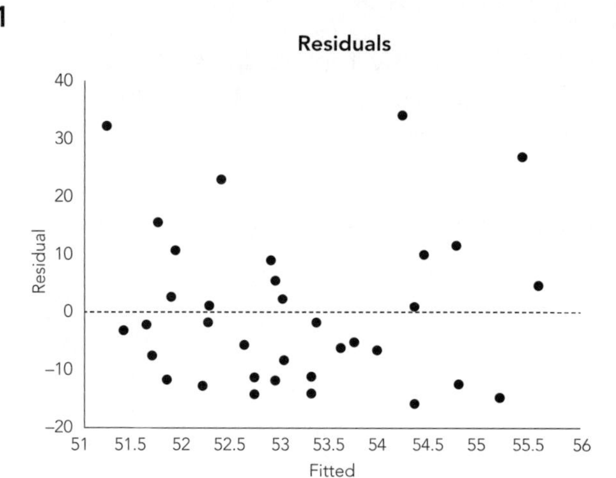

Observation: The residuals are/are not spread evenly above and below the horizontal axis.

Conclusion: Therefore a straight line/ curve is likely to be the best fit for this data set.

2

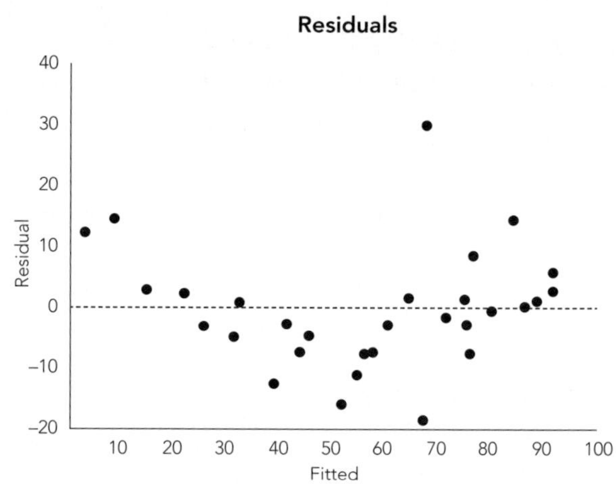

Observation: The residuals are/are not spread evenly above and below the horizontal axis.

Conclusion: Therefore a straight line/ curve is likely to be the best fit for this data set.

3

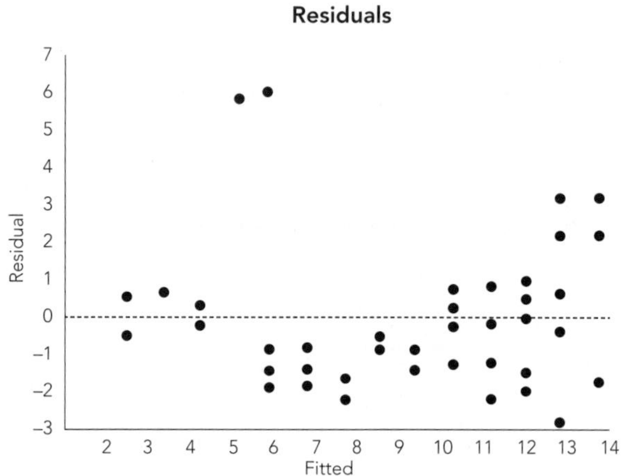

Observation: The residuals are/are not spread evenly above and below the horizontal axis.

Conclusion: Therefore a straight line/ curve is likely to be the best fit for this data set.

4

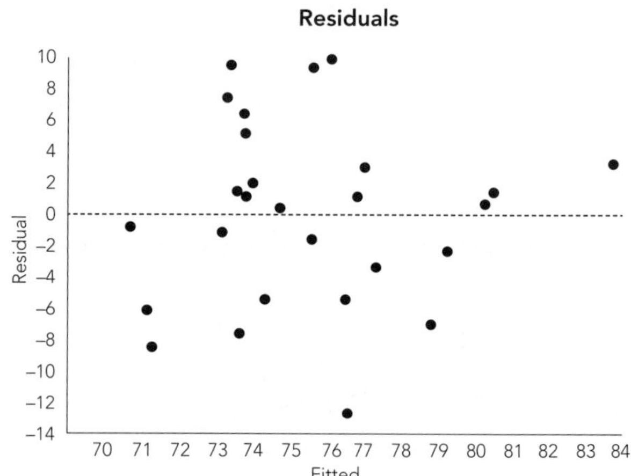

Observation: The residuals are/are not spread evenly above and below the horizontal axis.

Conclusion: Therefore a straight line/ curve is likely to be the best fit for this data set.

ISBN: 9780170462297

5

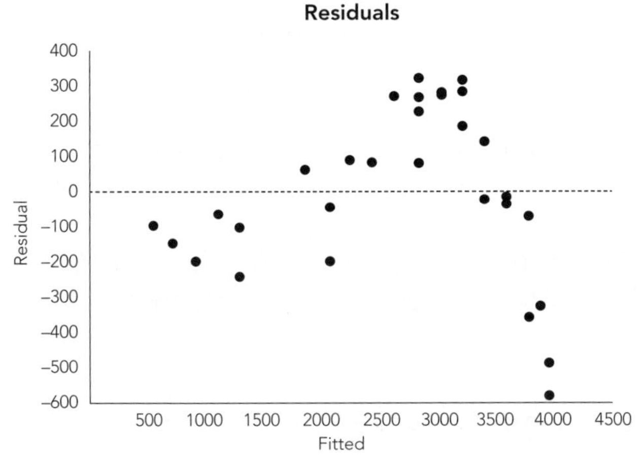

Observation: ______________________________

____

____

Conclusion: ______________________________

____

____

6

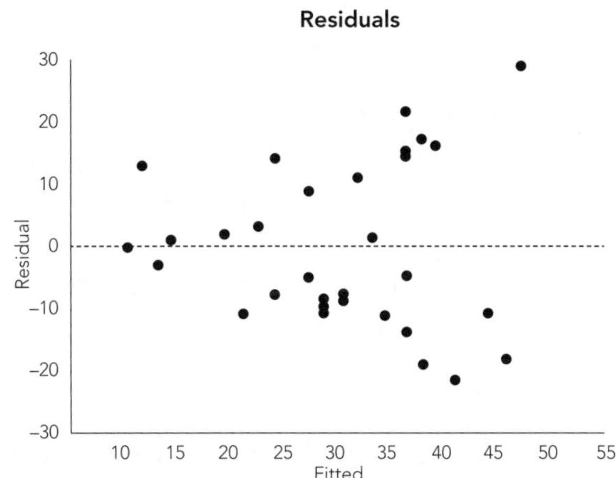

Observation: ______________________________

____

____

Conclusion: ______________________________

____

____

7

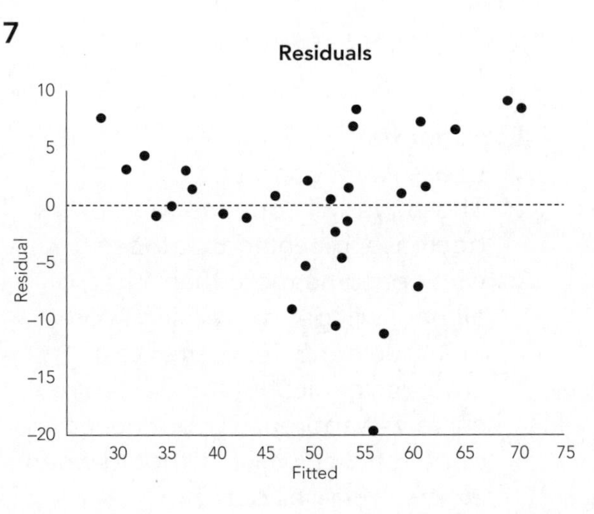

____

____

____

____

____

8

Residuals

Residual

10 8 6 4 2 0 −2 −4 −6 −8 −10

10 20 30 40 50 60 70

Fitted

____

____

____

____

____

ISBN: 9780170462297

D Fit a non-linear trend line

- Once again, your computer program will calculate the equations for you.
- You need to decide which curve fits by considering:
  1 Which **looks** the best fit.
  2 The data and the **context**, particularly the relationship between the data and the model at extreme values.
  For example:
  a Neither exponential curves nor logarithmic curves can pass through the point (0, 0).
  b Polynomials change direction, which may not be possible within the context.

Examples:

1 The relationship between the amount of alcohol consumed and dexterity.

Possible curves

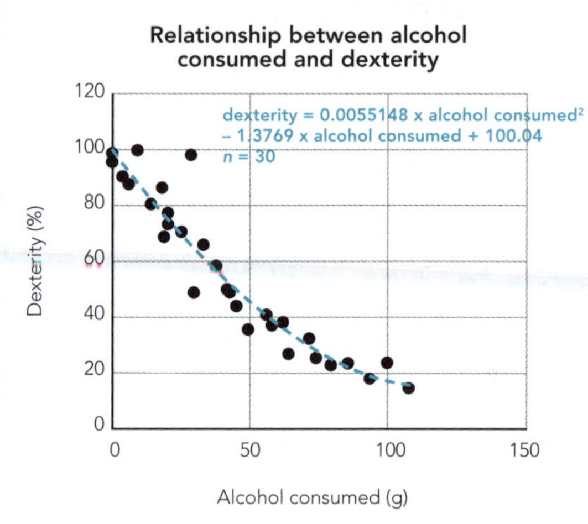

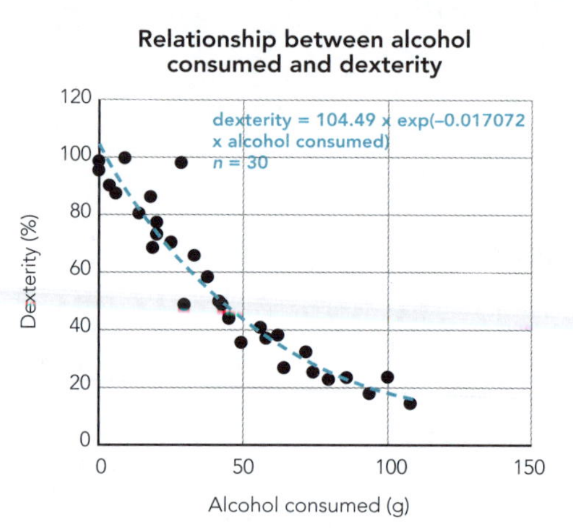

Quadratic

✓ Looks like a good fit.

≈ This fits well within the range of this data. However, because it is a parabola, the curve will eventually start to increase. This would mean that those who had consumed vast amounts of alcohol (more than 120 g) would have increasing scores in the dexterity test, which is very unlikely.

✓ 0 alcohol consumed ⇒ score = 100.04%, which is very close to 100%, the maximum possible score.

Exponential

✓ Looks like a good fit.

✓ The curve will continue to decrease, meaning that those who consume more than 110 g of alcohol will get decreasing scores in the dexterity test. After vast amounts of alcohol the dexterity curve will approach 0, but never quite reach it, which it should when a person passes out.

≈ 0 alcohol consumed ⇒ score = 104.49%, which is slightly higher than 100%, the maximum possible score.

Conclusion: The best fit for the data is the exponential curve, with the equation dexterity = 104.49 x exp(–0.017072 x alcohol consumed).

 ISBN: 9780170462297

2 The relationship between fish length and fish mass.

Possible curves

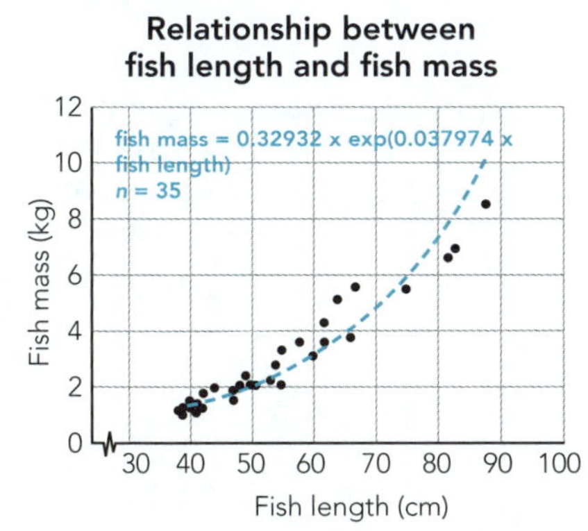

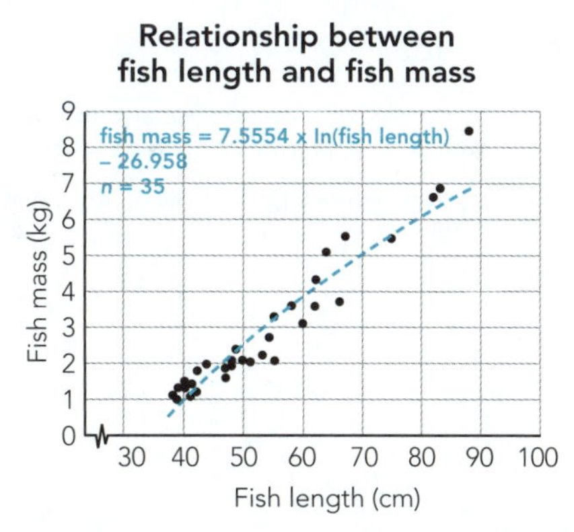

Exponential

≈ Moderately good fit, but not so good for longer fish.

✓ As fish get longer, they will continue to increase in mass.

✓ A fish with a length of 0 cm will have a mass of 0.32932 kg.

Logarithmic

✗ Poor fit, especially for the longest fish.

≈ As fish get longer, they will continue to increase in mass, but more slowly than the data suggests.

✗ Equation cannot be used for a mass of 0, and a 1 cm fish would have a mass of –26.958 kg, which is not possible.

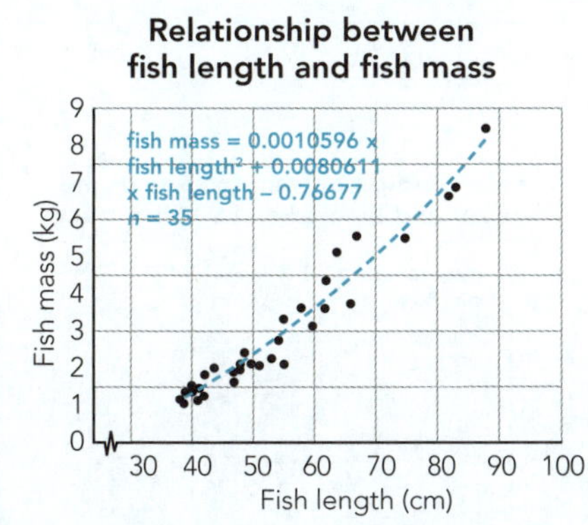

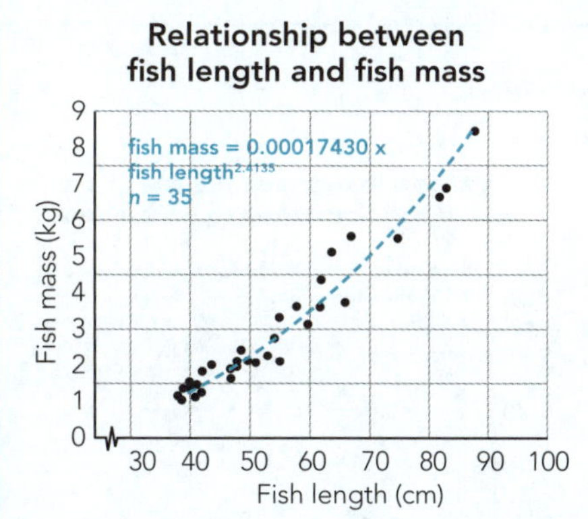

Quadratic

✓ Very good fit for the data.

✓ As fish get longer, they will continue to increase in mass.

✓ A fish with a length of 0 cm will have a mass of –0.76677 kg, which is not possible, but this is close to 0.

Power

✓ Very good fit for the data.

✓ As fish get longer, they will continue to increase in mass.

✓ A fish with a length of 0 cm will have a mass of 0.00017430 kg, which is very close to 0.

Conclusion: Both the quadratic (fish mass = 0.0010596 x fish length^2 + 0.0080611 x fish length – 0.76677) and the power model (fish mass = 0.00017430 x fish length$^{2.4135}$) would be very good models for this data.

ISBN: 9780170462297

Comment on each of the curves, and decide which fits best for each situation.

1 The relationship between the age of the walker and the time taken to walk a track.

Exponential

Relationship between the age of the walker and time taken to walk a track

time taken = 28.287 x exp(0.012695 x age)
n = 30

Time taken (minutes): 20, 30, 40, 50, 60, 70, 80, 90
Age (years): 0, 20, 40, 60, 80, 100

____

____

____

____

____

Logarithmic

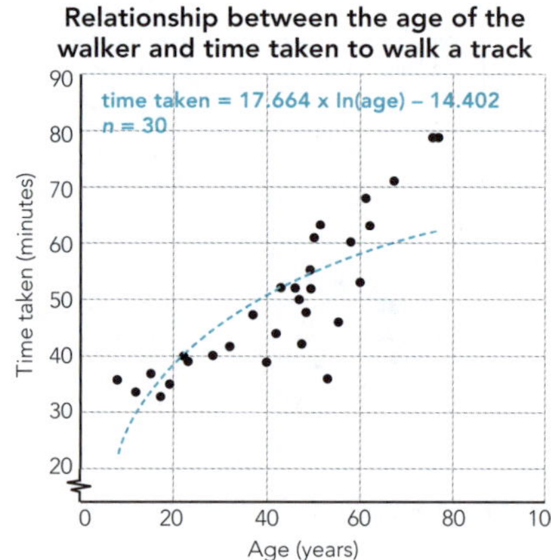

____

____

____

____

____

Quadratic

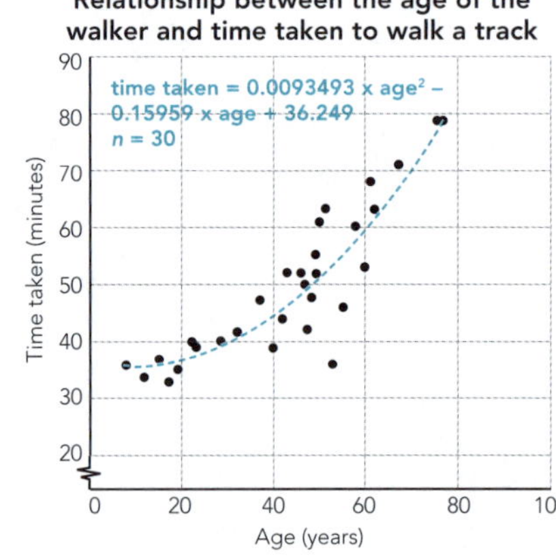

____

____

____

____

____

Power

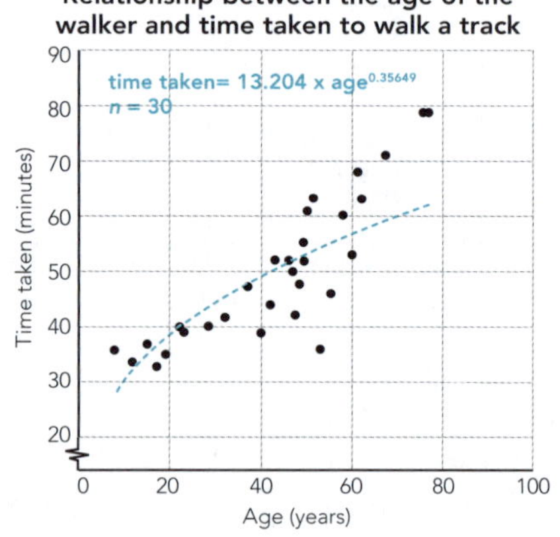

____

____

____

____

____

Best model: ______________________________

 ISBN: 9780170462297

2 The relationship between years of experience for an IT worker and salary.

Exponential

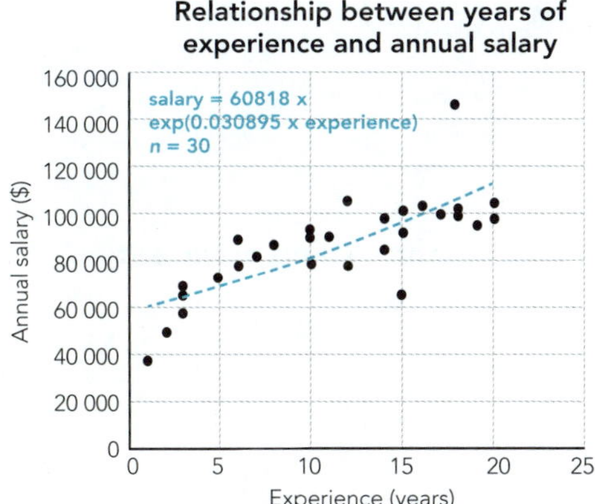

Logarithmic

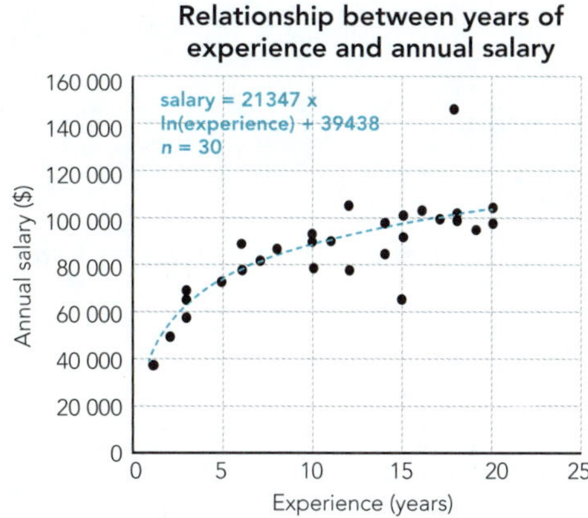

Quadratic

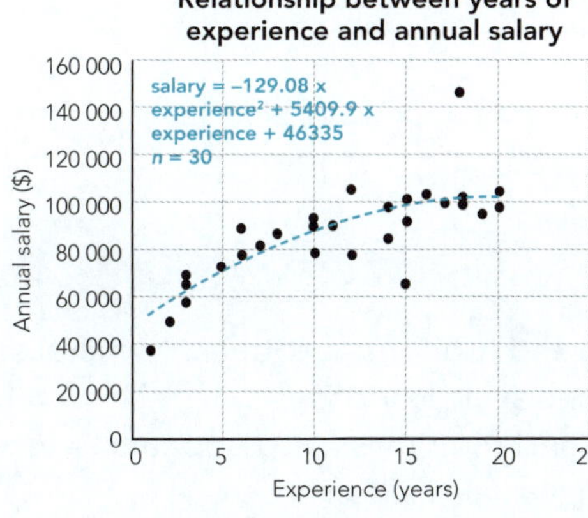

Power

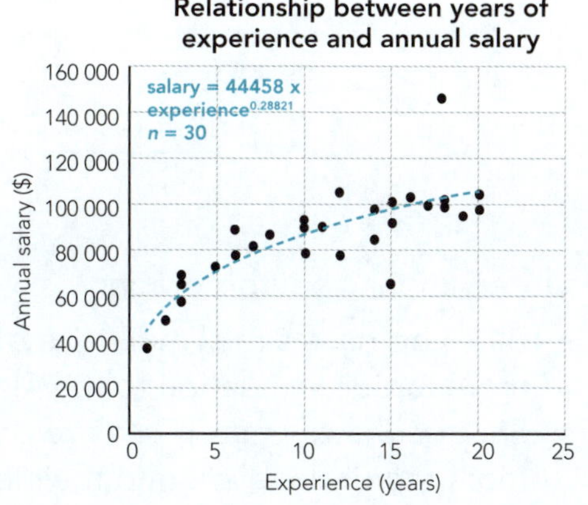

Best model: ______________________________

E Groupings

- These are subgroups within your data.
- Your computer program should allow you to distinguish groupings by using different colours or symbols (variable 3 on NZgrapher).
- You can separate the groups and analyse them individually.

Example:

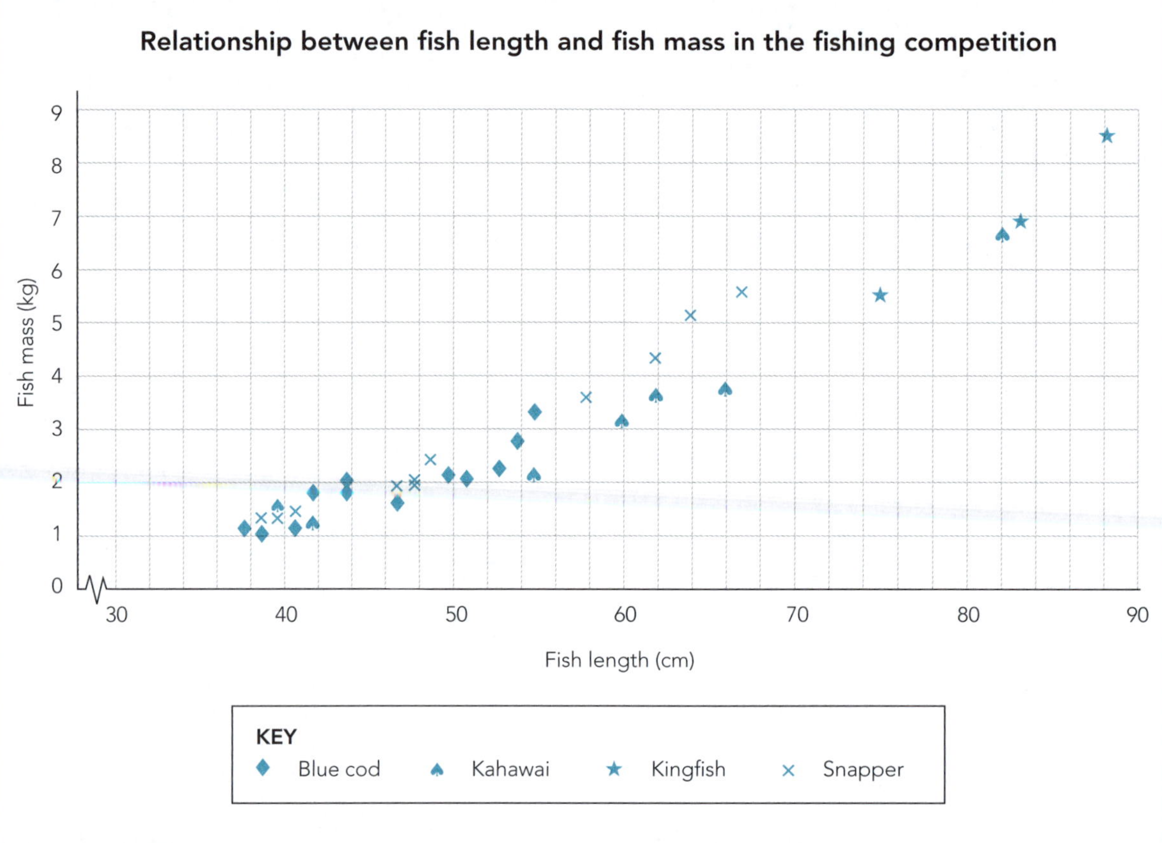

Observations from this graph:

- Blue cod have a maximum size of about 55 cm, and their mass appears to increase more rapidly in relation to their length than kahawai and kingfish.
- Snapper have a maximum size of about 68 cm, and their mass also appears to increase more rapidly in relation to their length than kahawai and kingfish.
- Kahawai have a maximum size of about 83 cm, and their mass appears to increase at a similar rate to kingfish, although kingfish are generally bigger.
- There were only three kingfish caught. These were some of the biggest fish caught in the competition, but there are too few data points to analyse on their own.

ISBN: 9780170462297

Separate analyses for blue cod, kahawai and snapper

Note that all of these numbers for all these species are too small for any major conclusions to be drawn.

Blue cod

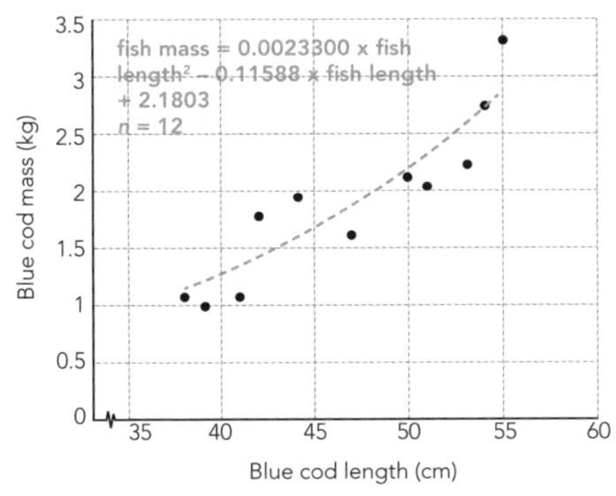

The quadratic model is the best fit for the relationship between length and mass of blue cod:

fish mass = 0.0023300 x fish length^2 – 0.11588 x fish length + 2.1803

Kahawai

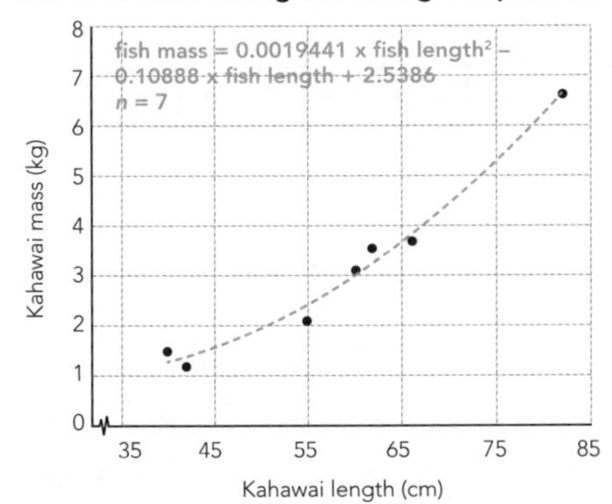

The quadratic model is also the best fit for the relationship between length and mass of kahawai:

fish mass = 0.0019441 x fish length^2 – 0.10888 x fish length + 2.5386

Snapper

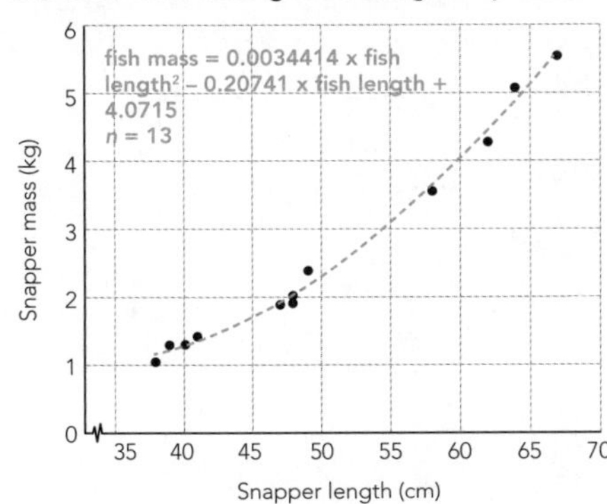

The quadratic model is also the best fit for the relationship between length and mass of snapper:

fish mass = 0.0034414 x fish length^2 – 0.20741 x fish length + 4.0715

Research questions arising from these models:

1 Why is a quadratic model the best for all of these situations?

2 What is the significance of the different values for the coefficients of x^2 in these models?

ISBN: 9780170462297

F Correlation and causality

- If two variables are **correlated**, then a change in one variable is associated with a change in the other variable, e.g. ice cream consumption is associated with the number of drownings.
- If there is a **causal** relationship between two variables, then a change in one variable **causes** a change in the other variable, e.g. how much exercise you do affects your fitness.
- There are often **several factors** that each causes some change in a response variable.

That two variables are correlated does not mean that one causes the other.

When two variables are correlated, it is very important not to jump to the conclusion that the change in one variable **causes** the change in the other. You should just observe that they are related. Then you should do **research** in order to find more evidence about the relationship.

Proving causality is one of the more difficult statistical exercises. The only way is by performing an experiment in which similar groups are given different treatments, and then comparing the results. This is often not possible for ethical reasons, e.g. one could not take two groups and force one group to smoke cigarettes in order to prove that smoking causes cancer.

Correlation does not prove causality

Multiple causes of correlation

The media often attribute **one** factor as the cause of an effect, when in fact there are many contributing and often linked factors. Take, for example, the headline 'No breakfast affects students' performance' (*Wall Street Journal*). There is no doubt that levels of blood sugar and hunger influence the performance of a student. However, whether a child has breakfast is also strongly associated with factors such as poverty, which also influences performance at school, as would absenteeism.

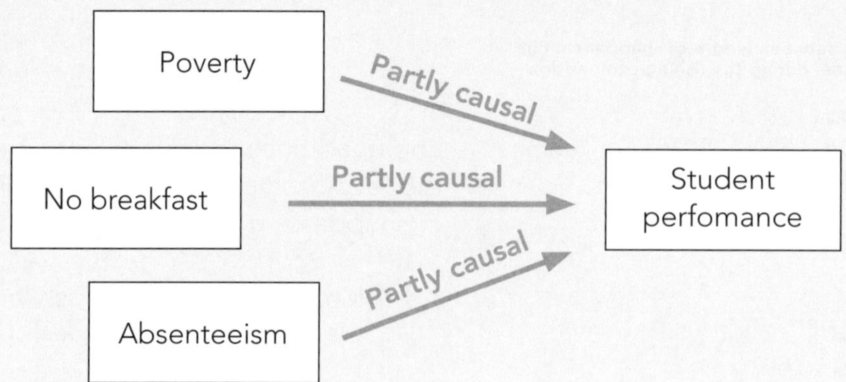

Writing about this:

It is likely that student performance is influenced in part by whether the student has had breakfast. However, other factors that could influence student performance are poverty and absenteeism.

ISBN: 9780170462297

Write sentences explaining the likely relationship between the variables.

1 Performance in sport is positively associated with athletic ability.

It is likely that performance in sport is influenced in part by ______________________.

However, other factors that are likely to influence performance in sport are

____.

2 Blue cod mass is positively associated with blue cod length.

It is likely that ______________________ is influenced in part by

______________________.

However, other factors that are likely to influence ______________________ are

____.

3 In the fishing competition, the length of the longest fish caught is positively associated with boat length.

____

____

____

4 The speed at which a person drives a car is positively associated with the tempo of the music they are listening to at the time.

____

____

____

Lurking variables

- A **lurking variable** is a variable that is not in the data set, but which is associated with changes in both the original variables. For example: ice cream consumption is associated with the number of drownings. Temperature is the lurking variable because when it is hot, more people buy ice cream and more people participate in water-based activities, so there are more drownings.

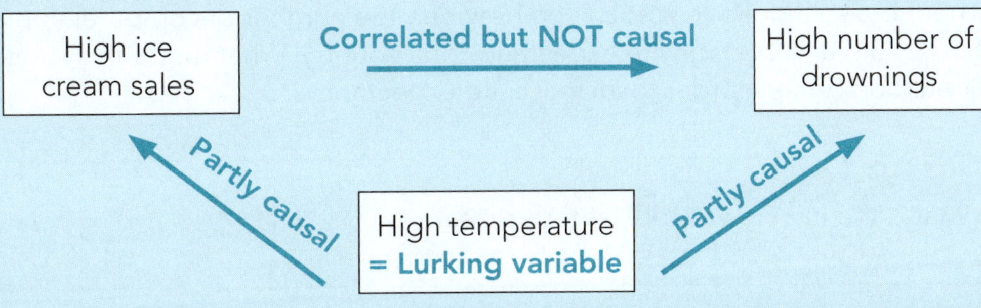

Lurking variables occur only where two variables are correlated, but there is no logical reason for one to influence the other.

ISBN: 9780170462297

Examples for discussion: Suggest what the lurking variable could be for the following pairs of positively correlated variables.

Explanatory variable	Response variable	Possible lurking variable
A child's shoe size	The child's mathematical ability	
Height	Salary	
Rates of obesity	Average age of car	
Number of civil engineering doctorates in the US	Consumption of mozzarella cheese in the US	

Answer the following questions.

5 **a** There is a positive association between the total volume of alcohol consumed and the number of serious crimes committed in a city. What might this suggest should be done in order to reduce the number of serious crimes?

b There is also a positive association between the total volume of milk consumed and the number of serious crimes committed in a city. What might this suggest should be done in order to reduce the number of serious crimes?

c What is the lurking variable in both cases?

6 **a** There is a positive association between the number of doctors per person and average life expectancy of a country. What might this suggest should be done in order to increase life expectancy?

b There is also a positive association between the number of computers per household and average life expectancy of a country. What might this suggest should be done in order to increase life expectancy?

c What is the lurking variable in both cases?

ISBN: 9780170462297

Writing about bivariate data

When writing about bivariate data, there are very few situations in which you can be definite about what you are stating. Here are some where you can:

Examples:

1 ✗ There **tends to be** a positive linear relationship between the length and mass of fish caught.

✓ There **is** a positive linear relationship between the length and mass of fish caught.

2 ✗ The equation of the linear model for the relationship between the length (x) and mass (y) of fish caught **is about** $y = 0.13518x - 4.3407$.

✓ The equation of the linear model for the relationship between the length (x) and mass (y) of fish caught **is** $y = 0.13518x - 4.3407$.

In nearly all situations, you should avoid definite statements.

Examples:

1 ✗ The positive linear relationship between the length and mass of fish caught means that longer fish **are** heavier.

✓ The positive linear relationship between the length and mass of fish caught means that longer fish **tend to be** heavier.

2 ✗ Because the linear model for the relationship between the length and mass of fish caught is $y = 0.13518x - 4.3407$, a 1 cm increase in fish length **will mean that** the mass of the fish will increase by 0.13518 kg.

✓ Because the linear model for the relationship between the length and mass of fish caught is $y = 0.13518x - 4.3407$, a 1 cm increase in fish length **will mean that on average**, the mass of the fish will increase by 0.13518 kg.

You should also be careful to match the strength of your statements to the situation.

Examples:

1 ✗ Removal of the unusual point results in a **slight** increase in the r value, which means the data is **a lot** closer to the trend line.

✓ Removal of the unusual point results in a **slight** increase in the r value, which means the data is **a little** closer to the trend line.

2 ✗ **r = 0.81**, so there is a **very strong** relationship between the two variables.

✓ **r = 0.81**, so there is a **strong** relationship between the two variables.

ISBN: 9780170462297

Select which is best from each pair of **blue** terms or phrases.

1 As the number of car drivers increases, the number of road deaths **tends to/will** increase.

2 r is close to 1, so there **is/tends to be** a positive association between the variables.

3 There is an unusual point in this data set. This **has/may have** been caused by a mistake in the data collection.

4 The linear model for the relationship between the body mass of an animal and its brain mass is $y = 1.5196x + 61.585$. If the body mass increases by 1 kg, the brain mass **will/is likely to** increase by **exactly/approximately** 1.5196 grams.

5 This is indicated by the slight increase in the r value, which means the data is **marginally/much** closer to the trend line.

6 Because r is close to 1, if I substitute body size into my equation, I **will/should** be able to make accurate predictions for brain size.

7 This means that the model **is not/may not be** applicable to animals smaller than a house mouse.

8 This data shows that if the body mass of a species increased by 5 kg, we would **see/expect** an increase in brain mass of 69 grams.

9 When working out an extrapolation, the second graph is **less suitable/flawed**.

10 This residual graph also **shows/suggests** that the linear model **will be/is likely to be** the most appropriate.

11 The best fit for the data **tends to be/is** the exponential curve, with the equation $y = 103.79\,e^{-0.017x}$.

12 r = 0.95, so my prediction **is/is likely to be** reliable.

13 I **can/cannot** be certain that this extrapolated value is accurate because I **can/cannot** assume that the trend will continue.

14 The equation $y = -0.9578x + 16.611$ describes the relationship between a child's age (x) and the length of time taken (y) to do a puzzle. The relationship **tends to be/is** negative.

ISBN: 9780170462297

Pick the errors

The following statements have errors or significant omissions. Identify these.

1 The dots are close to the line, so this means that as one variable increases, so does the other.

2 From this graph, we can see that there is a relationship between the body mass (kg) and the brain mass (g) of animals.

3 I changed my linear graph to a quadratic graph because it has a more accurate trend line.

4 The graph has an r value of 0.38 instead of 0.53, and the trend has therefore changed from a moderately strong relationship to having no relationship between variables.

5 The elephant is considered an unusual point because it has an extreme body mass compared to its brain mass.

6 There is a grouping on the graph, which means there is a constant scatter.

7 We can be reasonably confident that the interpolation prediction is accurate because it is on the line.

8 The graph shows how the number of drivers affects the number of deaths in the United States of America.

9 I am using a linear model because it fits the graph well and predicts the figures correctly.

ISBN: 9780170462297

Putting it all together

The following are the requirements for a basic report. These have been numbered in the report on pages 65–67.

1 Research your context.

2 Pose an appropriate question which is informed by contextual knowledge.

3 Identify and fully describe the response variable and the explanatory variable, with the units involved. Justify your choice.

4 State the purpose of your investigation and who would find it useful.

5 Plot the data. You **must** put the explanatory variable on the *x*-axis and the response variable on the *y*-axis.

6 Identify features in the data, i.e. positive or negative, linear or not, unusual points or groupings.

7 Fit a linear trend line, including the equation.

8 Describe the nature of the relationship, ideally using the gradient of the line.

9 Describe and justify the strength of the relationship.

10 Make at least one prediction. Include units and link them to the context.

11 Write a conclusion. Make sure it answers your question and link it to the purpose of your report.

Improving your report:

A Discussion and research on unusual points.

B Removal of unusual points, then re-analysis of model.

C Analyse the residuals graph.

D Fit a non-linear trend line.

E Discuss and analyse groupings if present, with research.

F Discuss correlation and causality, with research.

G Integrating research.

ISBN: 9780170462297

Relationship between girth and volume of *Pinus radiata*

Pinus radiata was introduced into New Zealand in the 1900s for forestry purposes (https://www.nzpcn.org.nz/flora/species/pinus-radiata/). It is the most popular commercial timber species in New Zealand, can grow to 150 years old and can reach to 2 m in diameter and 60 m high (https://www.nzffa.org.nz/farm-forestry-model/species-selection-tool/species/pine/radiata-pine/).

1 Research context.

Is there a relationship between girth (m) and the volume (m^3) of *Pinus radiata*, and if so, what is its nature. Can this be used to predict the volume of wood from a tree of a given girth? This would be useful for estimating the volume of wood that could be obtained from a tree by measuring its girth. Measuring girth is a simple thing to do in order to make the decision about whether or not a tree is ready to be chopped down for timber, whereas calculating its volume would be very difficult.

2 Appropriate question.

I will make the explanatory variable the girth of the tree in metres and the response variable the volume in cubic metres because measuring the girth could be useful for estimating the volume of wood in the tree.

3 Explanatory and response variables identified.

Foresters may be interested in the information from this report. It could be useful to estimate the volume of wood from the girth of the tree. This may give an insight into when is the optimal time for harvesting.

4 Purpose.

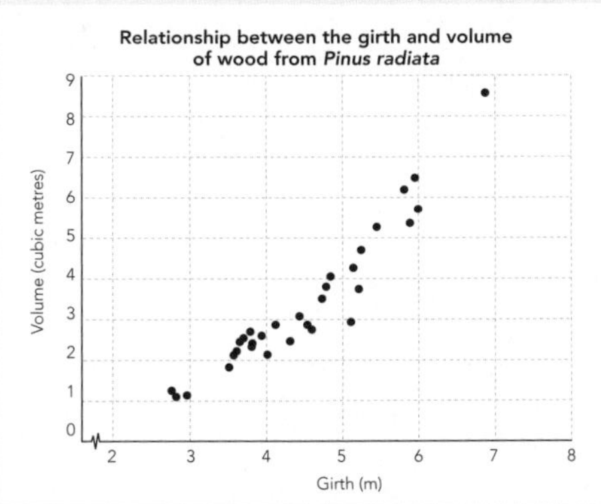

There is a strong positive, reasonably linear relationship between the girth of a *Pinus radiata* tree and its volume. This means that trees with bigger girths contain more wood. There is one unusual point: a very big tree with a girth of 6.87 m and a volume of 8.56 cubic metres.

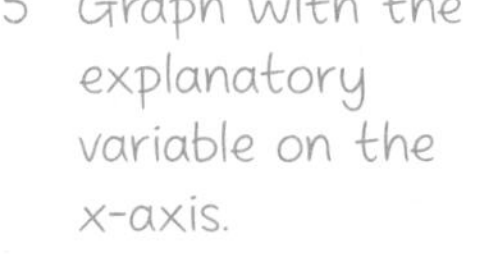

6 Identify features.

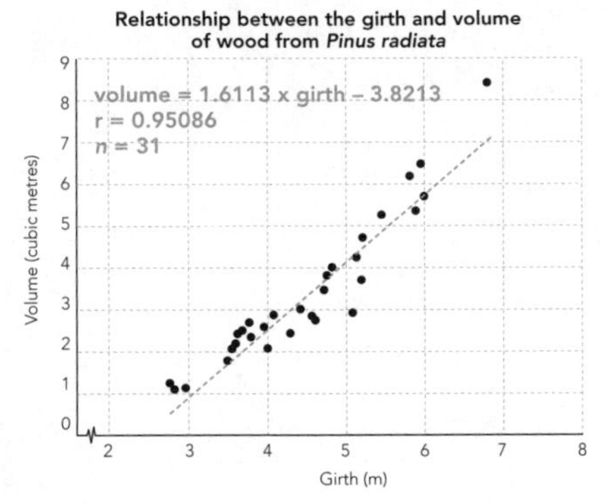

On average, an increase in girth of 1 metre is associated with an increase in wood volume of 1.6113 cubic metres.

I believe the relationship is very strong because most points are close to the line of best fit and the r value is 0.95086, which is very close to 1. The positive relationship shows that fatter trees tend to have a greater volume of wood.

7 Fit a linear trend line.

8 Describe the nature with the gradient.

9 Describe and justify strength.

Predictions:

Extrapolation: Using my linear model, I would expect a tree with a girth of 8 metres would have a volume of 9 (9.0691) cubic metres. We cannot have confidence in this prediction because 8 metres is more than a metre bigger than the girth of the largest tree. Also, we are assuming that the linear model continues, but the points for the two trees with the largest volumes both lie above the straight line of best fit.

10 Predictions made, linked to context, with units and appropriate rounding.

Interpolation: Using my linear model, I would expect a tree with a girth of 5 metres would have a volume of 4.2 (4.235) cubic metres. As an interpolation, this estimate should be reasonably accurate. However, most data values for trees with a girth of about 5 m lie below the regression line. Therefore, this prediction is likely to be an overestimate.

Unusual point

The point (6.87, 8.56) represents a tree which has a girth that is at least 0.87 m larger and a volume that is about 2 m^3 greater than any other tree. Because this tree is so much bigger than any other in the study, I will re-analyse the data without it. (At this point you should do some research on how large *Pinus radiata* trees grow.)

A Unusual point.

Improve the model

1 Remove the unusual point (6.87, 8.56).

B Improve the model by removing unusual point.

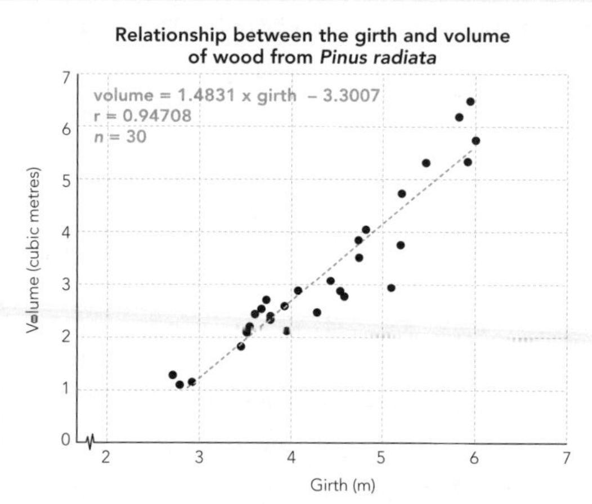

The r value (0.94708) is slightly less than that for our initial linear model, and points for five of the six biggest trees lie above this line. Consequently, I do not feel that removing the unusual point has improved the model.

2 Fit a curve if appropriate.

Residuals

C Analyse residuals.

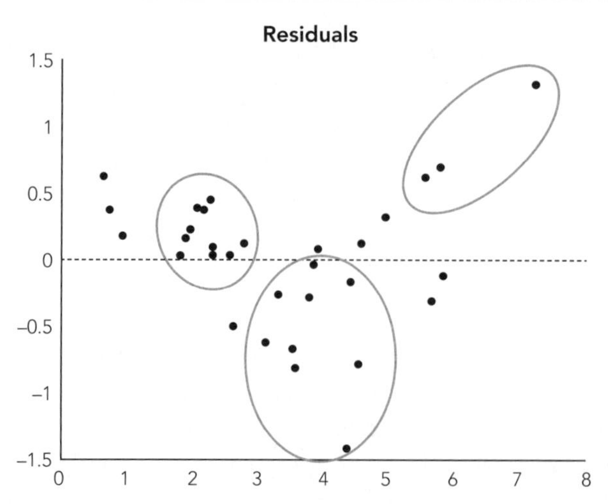

ISBN: 9780170462297

The distribution of positive residuals is not very even, with few positive values lying between girths of 4 and 5 metres. All the negative residuals are for girths between 4 and 6 metres. This suggests that a non-linear model might be more appropriate for this data.

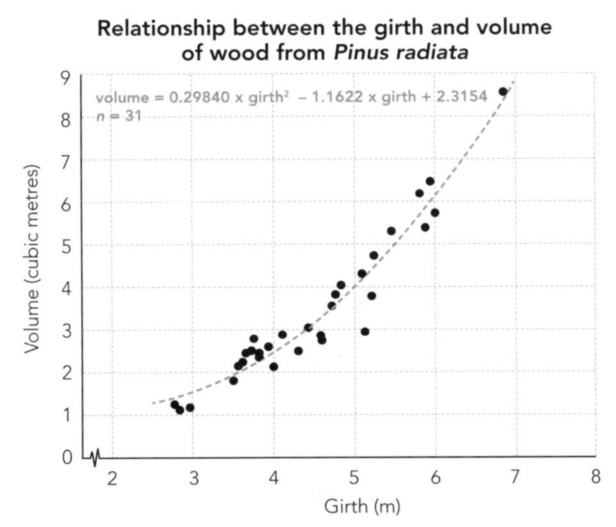

D Fit a non-linear trend line.

I believe that this quadratic model fits the data better than the linear one. The points, in particular those for bigger trees, are closer to the line of best fit. Volumes of wood for the three smallest trees are slightly below the quadratic line, though.

Prediction using the quadratic model: I would expect that a tree with a girth of 8 metres would have a volume of 12.12 cubic metres. This seems a much more feasible value for a tree with a girth of 8 metres than the linear prediction of 9.07 cubic metres.

Correlation and causality

I believe that there is likely to be a causal relationship between girth and volume of wood. Fatter trees are likely to be taller (research this). However, other factors that could influence the volume of wood are the height of the tree, how branched it is, etc.

F Correlation and causality.

Conclusion:

The relationship between the girth of *Pinus radiata* trees and their volume appears to be a quadratic relationship, because the best model for the data was volume = 0.29840 x girth^2 – 1.1622 x girth + 2.3154.

I think this quadratic model would work well for predicting the volume of wood that could be obtained from these trees. However, it may not be accurate for much bigger trees, nor for other species, and it may not apply to *Pinus radiata* trees growing in different conditions, or at different locations.

11 Conclusion, which is linked to the purpose.

Overall, this means that the volume of a *Pinus radiata* tree increases in proportion to the square of the girth, and the volume of wood obtained from a tree can be reasonably accurately obtained by measuring the girth (by using the equation above) before the tree is cut down.

This study could be improved by increasing the number of trees measured, and repeating it at a variety of locations, and with different species.

ISBN: 9780170462297

Practice tasks

Practice task one

Find the seven major mistakes or omissions from this report. Identify each and write a corrected version for each.

For our bodies to grow we need to feed them energy. Energy comes from fat, protein and carbohydrates. Fat contains more energy than protein or carbohydrates. (https://nutritionfoundation.org.nz/nutrition-facts/nutrients/energy)

What is the relationship between fat (g) and energy (Kj)? This data is from MegaBun. I am using fat as the response variable and energy as the explanatory variable. This study would be of interest to dieticians and customers concerned about their energy intake.

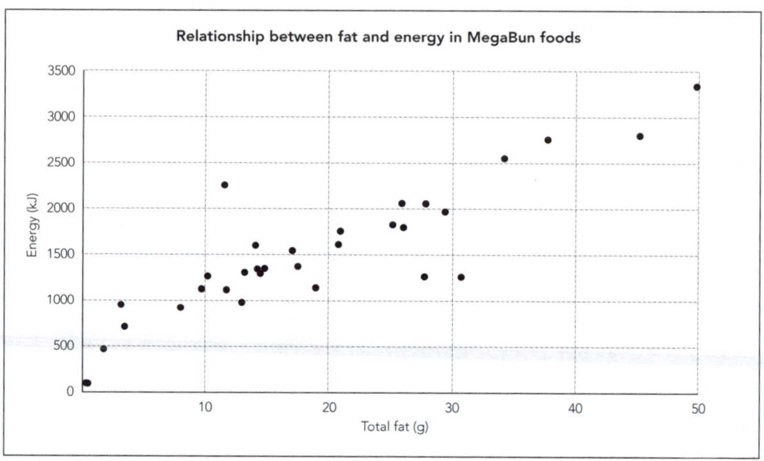

From the graph above we can tell that there is a moderately strong positive relationship between fat and energy in MegaBun products. This suggests that as the total fat increases, the energy levels decrease. There are no unusual points.

There is a fairly constant scatter. The r value (52.355) is reasonably high which means that most data points lie quite close to the linear trend line.

The gradient tells us that for an increase of 1 gram of fat we would expect to see an increase of 514.48 kj of energy. The more fat a MegaBun product has, the more energy it has.

I predict that that an item of MegaBun food with 20 g of fat should have 532.62 kJ of energy.

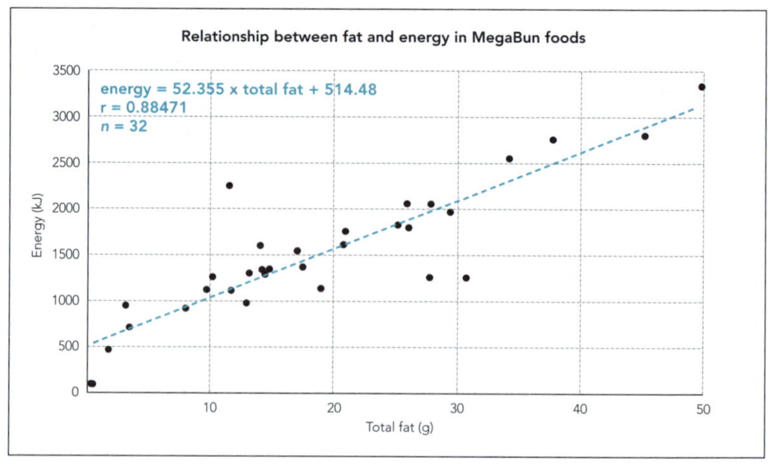

In conclusion I think that there is a moderately strong positive linear relationship between energy and fat in MegaBun's foods.

ISBN: 9780170462297

1

2

3

4

5

6

7

ISBN: 9780170462297

Practice task two

Thirty male university students all drank beer over a two-hour period. The volume of beer (litres) drunk by each was recorded. At the end of the two hours, each was given a breathalyser test. The results were recorded in micrograms of alcohol per litre of breath.

(An electronic version of this data can be found at cengage.co.nz/39BivariateData.)

This activity requires you to carry out a bivariate data investigation using the given variables and to write a report of your findings.

Use the statistical enquiry cycle to carry out a statistical investigation to determine if there is a relationship between at least one pair of variables.

Write a report describing the investigation.

1. Familiarise yourself with the data set provided. This will include doing research to help you understand the variables and develop a purpose for the investigation.
2. Pose an appropriate relationship question that can be answered using variables in the data set.
3. Identify features in the data, including the nature and strength of the relationship.
4. Use your model to make a prediction or predictions.
5. Write a conclusion answering your question.
6. Support your conclusion by referring to your analysis and/or features of the visual display(s). Include a reflection on your process, which could consider other relevant variables, or evaluate the adequacy of your model(s).

In writing your report, link your discussion to the context and support the statements you make by referring to statistical evidence.

ISBN: 9780170462297

Data:

Name	Volume drunk (mL)	Breathalyser reading (mcg alcohol/L breath)
Fergus	200	25
Bob	300	0
Andy	300	15
Michael	330	20
Sandy	450	45
Mitch	500	70
Joel	600	80
Frank	600	105
Sam	630	125
Will	660	55
Freddy	700	135
Patrick	750	85
Seone	900	330
Mark	900	205
Angus	900	127

Name	Volume drunk (mL)	Breathalyser reading (mcg alcohol/L breath)
Neil	960	270
Alex	990	115
Tane	990	215
Henare	1000	300
Tom	1200	480
Jarrod	1200	280
Rob	1200	255
Dave	1320	290
Iosefa	1320	395
Charlie	1500	520
Ron	1500	335
Russel	1600	580
Jason	1650	365
Tim	1650	405
Kahu	1800	620

Research:

ISBN: 9780170462297

Question:

____

____

____

____

Variables:

Explanatory variable: ______________________________

Response variable: ______________________________

Reason for choice: ______________________________

____

____

____

____

Purpose:

____

____

____

____

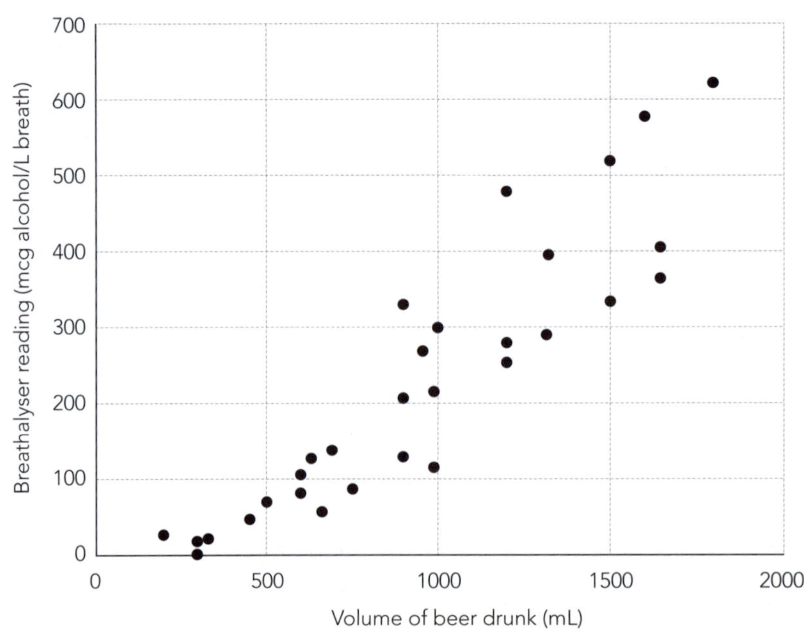

ISBN: 9780170462297

Features:

____

____

____

____

____

____

Relationship between volume of beer drunk by male university students in two hours and breathalyser reading

Describe nature:

____

____

____

____

____

____

Describe and justify strength:

____

____

____

____

____

____

ISBN: 9780170462297

Prediction(s):

Conclusion:

ISBN: 9780170462297

Practice task three

Records were kept for 32 people who bought indoor fitness machines during a three-year period:

Machine type: Stationary cycles, treadmills and rowing machines.
Price: The price they paid for their machine ($).
Ownership: How long they had owned the machine (months).
Time used during previous week: How long they had spent using the machine over the previous week (hours).

(An electronic version of this data can be found at cengage.co.nz/39BivariateData.)

This activity requires you to carry out a bivariate data investigation using at least two variables and to write a report of your findings.

Use the statistical enquiry cycle to carry out a statistical investigation to determine if there is a relationship between at least one pair of variables.

Write a report describing the investigation.

1 Familiarise yourself with the data set provided. This will include doing research to help you understand the variables and develop a purpose for the investigation.

2 Pose an appropriate relationship question that can be answered using variables in the data set. The variables you choose must be numerical, and the variable you use as your response variable must be continuous. You may choose to investigate more than one pair of variables. Select an appropriate display or displays to graph your data.

3 Identify features in the data, including the nature and strength of the relationship.

4 Find an appropriate model.

5 Use your model to make a prediction or predictions.

6 Write a conclusion answering your question.

7 Support your conclusion by referring to your analysis and/or features of the visual display(s). Include a reflection on your process, which could consider other relevant variables, or evaluate the adequacy of your model(s).

In writing your report, link your discussion to the context and support the statements you make by referring to statistical evidence.

ISBN: 9780170462297

Name	Machine type	Price ($)	Ownership (months)	Time used during previous week (hours)
Abi	Cycle	1650	15	8.5
Adam	Treadmill	2500	31	3.5
Annie	Rower	2200	21	2.75
Ash	Rower	2900	1	10.2
Bert	Rower	800	26	4
Darleen	Cycle	840	36	0
Didier	Treadmill	2300	8	6.5
Ellie	Rower	1200	8	3.75
Elspeth	Rower	500	18	0
Frank	Rower	150	36	2.5
Hannah	Rower	1130	32	1.75
Harry	Treadmill	1000	17	4.25
Jack	Cycle	1350	1	8
Jarrod	Treadmill	400	1	5.75
Jenny	Treadmill	900	4	3.5
John	Treadmill	1350	15	4
Lelei	Cycle	900	19	2.75
Leo	Cycle	200	28	1.25
Mac	Cycle	4100	3	6.25
Mae	Cycle	150	2	4.5
Ngaire	Rower	600	3	6
Nigel	Treadmill	700	25	2
Nikora	Rower	350	11	5.25
Penny	Treadmill	350	19	1
Peter	Cycle	550	5	6.5
Richie	Rower	1500	2	6.5
Rob	Treadmill	6500	2	9.25
Scott	Rower	450	27	0.75
Sophia	Cycle	1000	6	4
Stacey	Treadmill	3400	12	5.75
Tane	Treadmill	650	30	4.25
Tia	Cycle	750	10	3

ISBN: 9780170462297

If you don't have access to the data or a device, here are some graphs you could use to write a report.

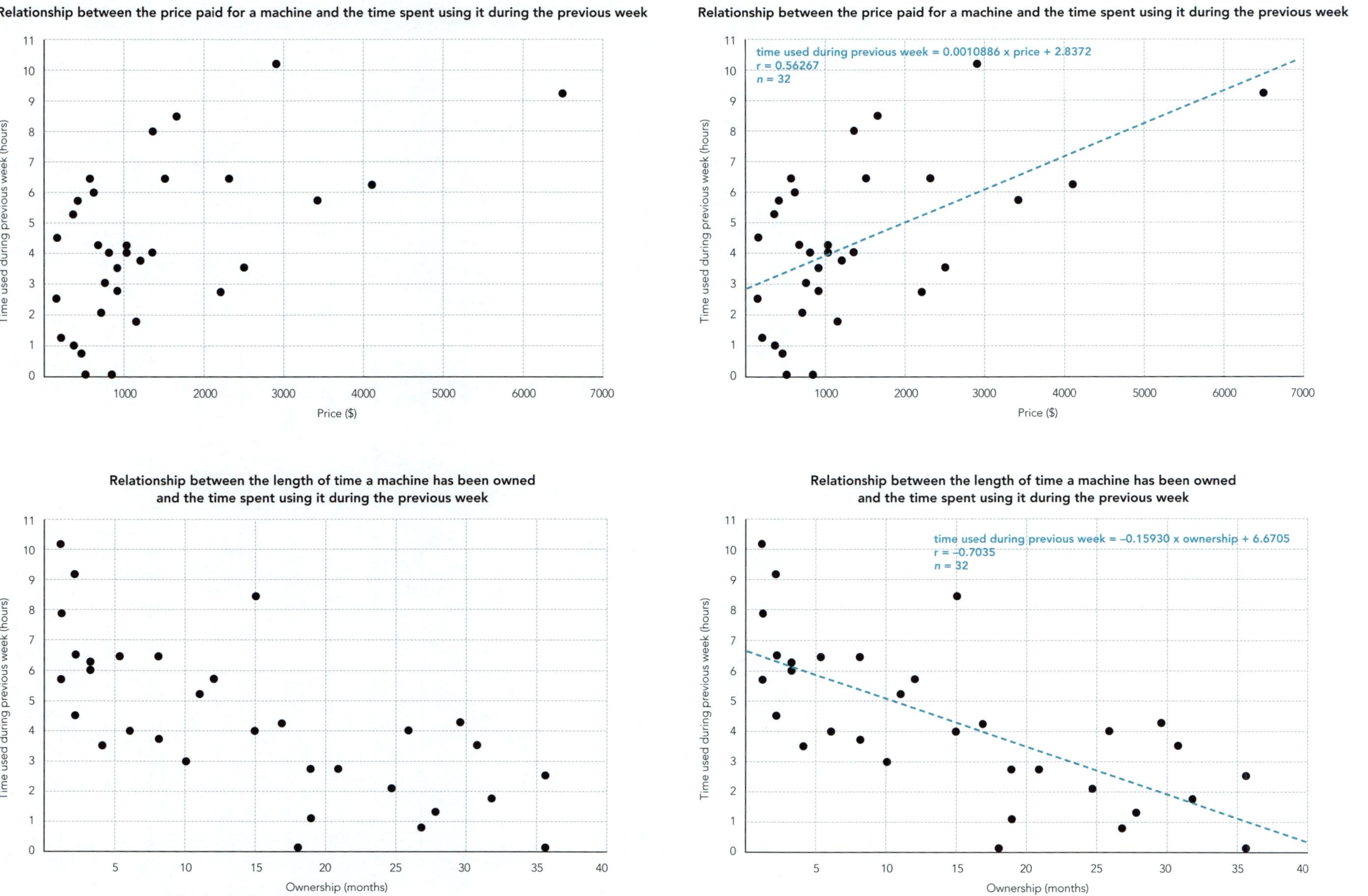

ISBN: 9780170462297

ISBN: 9780170462297

ISBN: 9780170462297

Answers

Variables (p. 7)

Variable	Type of variable	Suitable for a response variable?
Favourite colour	Descriptive	✗
Foot length	Continuous	✓
Number of pens in students' pencil cases	Discrete	✗
Head circumference	Continuous	✓
Clothing size (XS, S, M, etc.)	Descriptive	✗
Number of pets per family	Discrete	✗
Number of text messages on students' phones	Discrete	✗
Favourite ice-cream flavour	Descriptive	✗
Height	Continuous	✓
Size of your bedroom (m^2)	Continuous	✓
Distance travelled to school	Continuous	✓
Eye colour	Descriptive	✗
Arm span	Continuous	✓
Make of calculator	Descriptive	✗
Age	Continuous	✓

Possible answers. If you have others, check with your teacher.

Height	and	Head circumference
Height	and	Arm span
Age	and	Height
Age	and	Distance travelled to school
Arm span	and	Size of your bedroom (m^2) (although a relationship is unlikely)

Setting up your investigation (pp. 8–38)

1a Research your context (p. 10)

How are fishing competitions usually judged? By mass or length or number of different species?
Is there a limit to where boats can go?
Are there catch limits on species?
Are there limits to boat size? Or different categories of types of boats?
Possible websites:
https://www.mpi.govt.nz/fishing-aquaculture/recreational-fishing/
https://www.newzealandnow.govt.nz/resources/keep-your-catch-legal

1b Select suitable data (pp. 10–11)

1 No, it's not suitable because we don't have two bits of information about each fish.
2 It's possible to analyse this but given the relationship between the two variables is weak, it would be hard to write an insightful report.
3 Yes, but the relationship is not very strong.
4 Possible but it's unlikely that the age of the catcher would have anything to do with the boat length.
5 No, as the variable number of species caught on the *y*-axis is discrete.

2 Pose an appropriate question which is informed by context and knowledge (pp. 12–13)

1 **Good question?** No (implies relationship and no units)
Rewritten question: Is there a relationship between the mass (kg) and the height (cm) of the students in my statistics class, and if so, what is its nature?
2 **Good question?** No (units or population)
Rewritten question: Is there a relationship between leaf length (mm) and leaf width (mm) for rewarewa trees in the Tasman region, and if so, what is its nature?
3 **Good question?** No (can be answered with a yes or no.)
Rewritten question: Is there a relationship between the amount of fertiliser (g) and the mass (kg) of tomatoes produced by each plant in my garden, and if so, what is its nature?
4 **Good question?** Yes
5 Is there a relationship between the amount of alcohol consumed (g) and the dexterity (%) of students from Mansfield University, and if so, what is its nature?
6 Is there a relationship between the age of walkers (years) and the time taken to walk a track (minutes) for walkers from Humphrey's tramping club, and if so, what is its nature?

3 Name the response variable, name the explanatory variable, and justify your choice (pp. 14–16)

1 **Plant height:** Response
Amount of fertiliser applied: Explanatory
Reason: The amount of fertiliser is likely to be a factor in explaining the amount a plant grows.

ISBN: 9780170462297

The amount it it grows does not explain the amount of fertiliser added.

Plant height

Amount of fertiliser

How this information could be used: It could be useful to be able to predict the plant height from the amount of fertiliser used to see what the optimal amount will be.

2 **Age of car:** Explanatory
Value of car: Response
Reason: The age of a car will be a major factor in explaining its value. The value of a car does not explain its age.

Value of car

Age of car

How this information could be used: It could be useful to be able to predict the value of the car by the age of the car.

3 **Depth of river:** Response
Amount of rainfall: Explanatory
Reason: The amount of rain that falls is likely to have a major effect on how deep a river is. The depth of the river is unlikely to influence the amount of rainfall.

Depth of river

Amount of rainfall

How this information could be used: It could be useful to be able to predict the depth of the river from the amount of rain that has fallen.

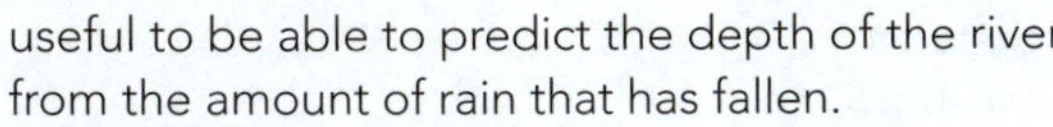

4 **Temperature:** Explanatory
Plant growth: Response
Reason: The temperature will certainly be one of the factors that affects how much a plant grows. The amount of plant growth will not affect how hot it is.

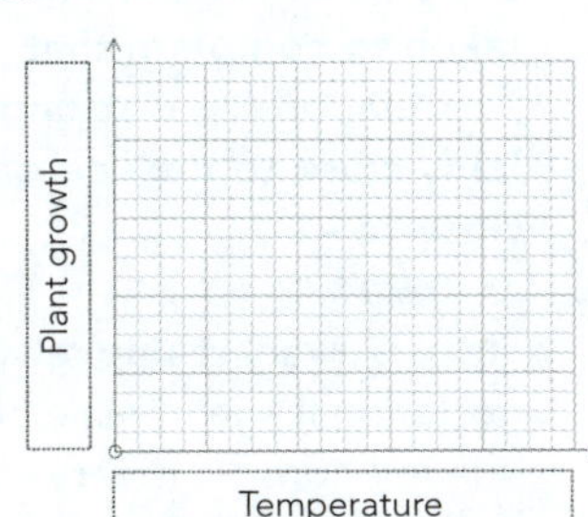

How this information could be used: It could be useful to look into what temperatures are optimal for plant growth.

5 **Stoat population:** Explanatory
Time spent stoat trapping: Response
Reason: Stoat population is discrete so it cannot be the response variable.

How this information could be used: It could be useful to be able to predict how much time will need to be spent trapping stoats from the population size.

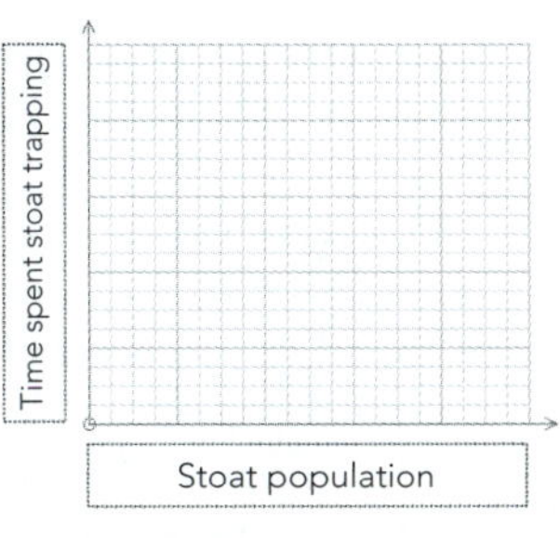

6 **A child's reading ability:** Response
A child's age: Explanatory
Reason: Age will be one of many factors that will explain reading ability.

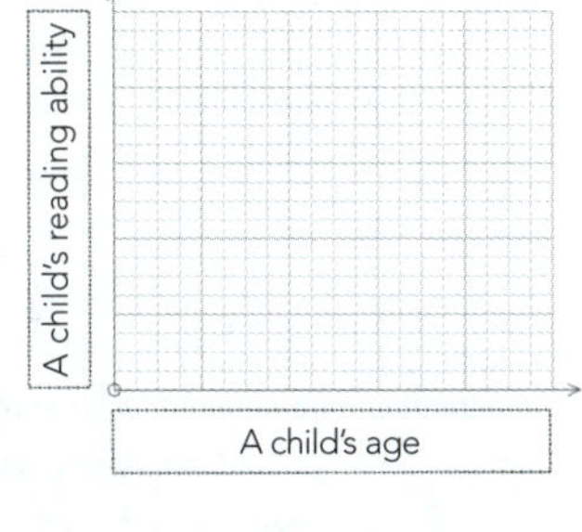

How this information could be used: It could be useful to be able to predict a child's reading ability from their age.

7 **Length of tramping track:** Explanatory
Time taken to walk it: Response
Reason: Length of the track will be one of several factors that will explain the time needed to walk it.

Time taken to walk

Length of tramping track

How this information could be used: It could be useful to be able to predict the time it will take to walk a tramping track by how long it is.

8 **Profit of ice creams sold:** Response
Air temperature: Explanatory
Reason: The air temperature will be one of the factors that will explain the ice cream vendor's profit.

Profit of ice creams sold

Air temperature

How this information could be used: The owner could predict their profit from the forecasted temperature.

4 State the purposed of your investigation and who would find it useful (pp. 17–18)

1 *Why might we investigate this:* To estimate how long walks take.
Who might be interested: Recreational trampers, Department of Conservation
What might you research: How fast people walk, How long does it take to walk tracks?

2 *Why might we investigate this:* To use it as a health indicator of babies, or consider natural/Caesarean deliveries.
Who might be interested: Expecting mothers, midwives, medical professionals, Plunket
What might you research: Does gestational time affect baby size?

6 Identify features in the data (pp. 20–22)

1 There is a **negative** relationship between **the amount of alcohol consumed** and **dexterity**. This means that as **the amount of alcohol consumed** increases, **dexterity** tends to **decrease**.
The relationship appears to be **non-linear**.
Other feature(s): There is one unusual point — a person who has consumed 29 g of alcohol and has a dexterity of 98%. Others with a similar amount of alcohol consumed had less dexterity.

2 There is a **positive** relationship between **the number of years' experience** and **salary**. This means that as **the number of years' experience** increases, **salary** tends to **increase**.
The relationship appears to be **non-linear**.
Other feature(s): There is one unusual point — a person who has 15 years' experience but a salary of only $64,000. This salary seems low compared to others with a similar amount of experience.

3 There is a **negative relationship between the person's age and the time taken to complete a puzzle**. This means that as **the age increases, the time taken to complete the puzzle tends to decrease**.
The relationship appears to be **non-linear**.
Other feature(s): There are two unusual points — aged 12 and 13 years old have taken 11–12 minutes to complete the puzzle. Others of a similar age completed it in less time.

4 There is a positive relationship between people's height and their arm span. This means as the height increases, their arm span tends to increase.
The relationship appears to be linear.
Other feature(s): There are two unusual points — a person with a small height and arm span which is away from the rest of the data, and the other who has a height of 171 cm but an arm span of only 152 cm (others who have a similar height have a larger arm span).

5 There is a negative relationship between the age of a car and its price.
This means that as a car's age increases, its price tends to decrease.
The relationship appears to be strong and non-linear.
Other feature(s): a group of older cars (27–30 years old) that are worth far more than cars of a similar age.

8 Describe the nature of the relationship (pp. 24–27)

1 m = **1.4765**
As **the length of the boat** increases by 1 **m**, we would expect the **length of the longest fish caught** to **increase** on average by **1.4765 cm**.

2 m = **0.85482**
As **the arm span of a Year 13 student** increases by 1 **cm**, we would expect the **height** to **increase** on average by **0.85482 cm**.

3 m = **–0.82689**
As **the amount of alcohol consumed** increases by **1 g**, we would expect the **dexterity** to **decrease** on average by **0.82689%**.

4 As the gestational age of a baby increases by 1 week, we would expect its mass to increase on average by 170.92 g.

5 As the age of a car increases by 1 year, we would expect the price of the car to decrease on average by $615.17.

6 As the experience of an IT worker increases by 1 year, we would expect their annual salary to increase on average by $2641.30.

9 Describe the strength of the relationship (pp. 28–32)

1 r = **0.53391**
There is a **moderately strong** relationship between **the length of the boat** and **the length of the longest fish caught**.
The relationship is **moderately strong** because **a number of points lie some distance from the line of best fit** and r is **not close to 1**.

2 r = **0.95351**
There is a **very strong** relationship between **arm span** and **height for Year 13 students**.
The relationship is **very strong** because **most points lie close to the line of best fit** and r is **very close to 1**.

3 r = **–0.86214**
There is a **strong relationship between age of the person completing the puzzle and the time taken to complete that puzzle**.
The relationship is **strong because most points lie fairly close to the line of best fit and r is fairly close to –1**.

4 r = **0.96622**
There is a **very strong relationship between the gestational age of male babies and their birth mass.**
The relationship is **very strong because most points lie very close to the line of best fit and r is very close to 1**.

ISBN: 9780170462297

5 r = –0.93504
There is a very strong relationship between the amount of alcohol consumed and the dexterity results for the adults. The relationship is very strong because most points lie very close to the line of best fit and r is very close to –1.

6 r = 0.76672
There is a strong relationship between the annual salary of IT workers and their number of years of experience. The relationship is strong because most points lie fairly close to the line of best fit and r is moderately close to 1. However, a non-linear model would probably fit better.

10 Use the model to make a prediction (pp. 33–38)

Note: Your estimates will vary — if you are not sure whether yours is reasonable, check with your teacher. Rounded values are given in brackets.

1 Interpolation
Estimate: Mass ≈ 3 kg
Calculation: Mass = 0.17915 x 12 + 0.97319
= 3.12299 kg
Observations:
1 The relationship is moderately weak.
2 We are estimating within the range of the data.
As a result: We are estimating within the range of the data, however the relationship is moderately weak. Therefore we would have little confidence in the prediction.

2 Interpolation
Estimate: Height ≈ 185 cm
Calculation: Height = 0.85482 x 190 + 23.240
= 185.6558 cm
Observations:
1 The relationship is very strong.
2 We are estimating within the range of the data.
As a result: We are estimating within the range of the data, and the relationship between arm span and height is very strong. Therefore we can have reasonable confidence in this prediction.

3 Extrapolation
Estimate: Time ≈ 1 min
Calculation: Time = –0.86542 x 18 + 16.309
= 0.73144 minutes
Observations: The relationship is strong. We are estimating beyond the range of the data. This means we are assuming that the linear relationship continues beyond the range of the data, which may not be the case. Depending on the complexity of the puzzle, there would be a limit as to how fast it could be completed.
As a result: The relationship is strong, and we are extrapolating only a short distance from the end of the data, so we can have reasonable confidence in this prediction.

4 Interpolation
Estimate: Birth mass ≈ 1990 g
Calculation: Birth mass = 170.92 x 32 – 3471.3
= 1998.14 g (1990 g)
Observations: The relationship is very strong. We are also estimating within the range of the data.
As a result: We would expect this estimate to be reasonably accurate.

5 Interpolation
Estimate: Dexterity score ≈ 19%
Calculation: Dexterity score = 17.2679% (17%)
Observations: The relationship is very strong. We are also estimating within the range of the data.
As a result: We would expect this estimate to be only reasonably accurate.

6 Extrapolation
Estimate: Salary ≈ $118 000
Calculation: Salary = $117 500 ($118 000)
Observations: The relationship is strong but we are estimating beyond the range of the data. Most data values near this are below the line of best fit.
As a result: The prediction is probably an over-estimate. A non-linear model would probably give a more accurate estimate.

Improving your report (pp. 42–60)

A An in-depth look at unusual points (pp. 42–44)

1 There are two unusual points:
(18, 145 000): This point is unusual because most people who have about 18 years' experience in the IT industry are earning about $100 000, and this person is earning $45 000 more than this. I would find out who this person was, who they were working for, and their role in the organisation.
(15, 62 000): This point is unusual because most people who have about 15 years' experience in the IT industry are earning a bit less than $100 000, but this person is earning about $30 000 less than this. I would find out who this person was, who they were working for, and their role in the organisation.

2 (3.5, 67): This point is unusual because most fish caught from small boats were under 45 cm. This fish was at least 20 cm bigger than other fish caught from small boats. This data was listed on page 9, and this fish was a snapper. Small boats do not tend to go far offshore. I would research snapper sizes, and find out if large snapper are likely to be found close to the shore.

3 There are two unusual points, one at (12, 12) and another at (13, 11). These points are unusual as children of a similar age completed the puzzle in around 4–5 minutes.

4 (29, 98). This point is unusual as they have consumed 29 g of alcohol and have 98% dexterity. Others with a similar consumption have a dexterity of around 65%.

ISBN: 9780170462297

B By removing unusual points (pp. 45–46)

1. The slope of the line of best fit changes from **2641.3** to **2472.4**.
   This means that **for an increase of one year's experience for an IT worker, we would expect to see an increase in salary of $2641.30. This compares with $2472.40 without the unusual points.**
   The r value increases from **0.76672** to **0.85433**.
   This means that **the data without the unusual points, on average, lies closer to the line of best fit.**
2. The slope of the line of best fit changes from 1.4765 to 1.7003.
   This means that an increase of 1 m in boat length is associated with an increase of 1.4765 cm in the length of the longest fish caught in the fishing competition. This compares with an increase of 1.7003 cm without the unusual point.
   The r value increases from 0.53391 to 0.60571.
   This means that the data without the unusual point, on average, lies closer to the line of best fit.

C Analyse the residual graph (pp. 47–51)

How residuals are calculated

1

2

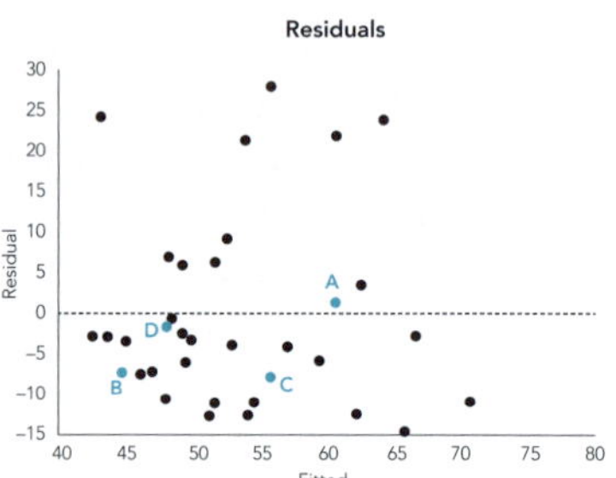

3

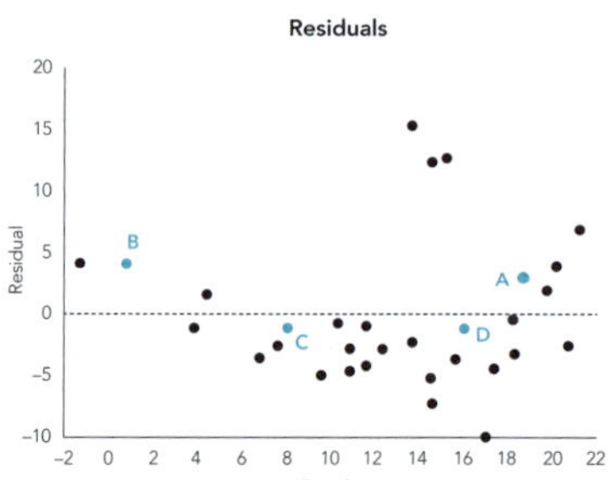

Interpreting residuals

1. **Observation:** The residuals **are** spread evenly above and below the horizontal axis.
   Conclusion: Therefore a **straight line** is likely to be the best fit for this data set.
2. **Observation:** The residuals **are not** spread evenly above and below the horizontal axis.
   Conclusion: Therefore a **curve** is likely to be the best fit for this data set.
3. **Observation:** The residuals **are not** spread evenly above and below the horizontal axis.
   Conclusion: Therefore a **curve** is likely to be the best fit for this data set.
4. **Observation:** The residuals **are** spread evenly above and below the horizontal axis.
   Conclusion: Therefore a **straight** line is likely to be the best fit for this data set.
5. **Observation:** The residuals are not spread evenly above and below the horizontal axis.
   Conclusion: Therefore a curve is likely to be the best fit for this data set.
6. **Observation:** The residuals are spread evenly above and below the horizontal axis.
   Conclusion: Therefore a straight line is likely to be the best fit for this data set.
7. **Observation:** The residuals are not spread evenly above and below the horizontal axis.
   Conclusion: Therefore a curve is likely to be the best fit for this data set.
8. **Observation:** The residuals are not spread evenly above and below the horizontal axis.
   Conclusion: Therefore a curve is likely to be the best fit for this data set.

D Fit a non-linear trend line (pp. 52–55)

1 **Exponential**

≈ Reasonable fit, but not so good for older people.

≈ A baby (0 years) would take 29 minutes to walk track, which is not feasible. Two-, three- and four-year-olds would all take 36 minutes, which is reasonable.

✗ Poor fit at higher values.

Logarithmic

✗ Poor fit.

✗ A 1-year-old would take –14 minutes to walk track, which is not possible.

✗ Very poor fit at higher values.

Quadratic

✓ Good fit.

≈ A baby would take about 36 minutes, which is not feasible. Two-, three- and four-year-olds would also take 36 minutes, which is reasonable.

✓ For older people, the time taken increases with age, which would fit with reality.

ISBN: 9780170462297

Power

✗ Poor fit.

✗ A baby (0 years) would take 13 minutes to walk track, which is not possible.

✗ Very poor fit at higher values.

Best model: Quadratic model $y = 0.0093x^2 - 0.1596x + 36.249$

2 **Exponential**

✗ Poor fit.

✗ A person with no experience would start on a salary of $57 443, which seems unlikely.

✗ Salaries increase at an increasing rate as a person gets more experience.

Logarithmic

✓ Very good fit.

✓ The model does not work for a person with no experience, but a person with one year's experience would get a salary of $39 422, which seems reasonable compared with actual values.

✓ Salaries continue to increase as a person gains more experience, but at a decreasing rate.

Quadratic

✓ Good fit except at lower values.

✗ A person with no experience would start on a salary of $46 305, which seems rather high compared with actual values.

✗ For people with more experience, the model fits well, but because it is a quadratic, salaries for the most experienced people will eventually decline, which does not seem likely.

Power

✓ Very good fit.

✗ A person with no experience would start on a salary of $44 447, which seems rather high compared with actual values.

✓ Salaries continue to increase as a person gains more experience, but at a decreasing rate.

Best model: Logarithmic model $y = 21\,362\ln(x) + 39\,422$

F **Correlation and causality (pp. 58–60)**

1 It is likely that performance in sport is influenced in part by **athletic ability**.
However, other factors that are likely to influence performance in sport are **attitude, amount of training done, teamwork, quality of coaching, etc.**

2 It is likely that **blue cod mass** is influenced in part by **blue cod length**.
However, other factors that are likely to influence **blue cod mass** are **the amount of food available, gender, whether the fish is carrying eggs or not, etc.**

3 It is likely that the length of the longest fish caught is influenced in part by boat length. However, other factors that are likely to influence the length of the longest fish caught are the number of people fishing on the boat, the location of fishing, etc.

4 It is likely that the speed at which a person drives is influenced in part by the tempo of the music they are listening to at the time. However, other factors that are likely to influence the speed at which a person drives are the person's age, the volume of music, the type of music, the type of car, etc.

Lurking variables

Explanatory variable	Response variable	Possible lurking variable
A child's shoe size	The child's mathematical ability	**The age of the child**
Height	Salary	**Gender — on average, males are paid more than females for equivalent jobs**
Rates of obesity	Average age of car	**Wealth of the country.**
Number of civil engineering doctorates in the US	Consumption of mozzarella cheese in the US	**Wealth – both are associated with increased standards of living**

5 a Reduce the total volume of alcohol consumed.
b Reduce the total volume of milk consumed.
c Population of the city.

6 a Increase the number of doctors per person.
b Increase the number of computers per household.
c Wealth of the country.

Writing about bivariate data (pp. 61–62)

1 As the number of drivers increases, the number of road deaths **tends to** increase.

2 r is close to 1, so there **is** a positive association between the variables.

3 There is an unusual point in this data set. This **may have** been caused by a mistake in the data collection.

4 The linear model for the relationship between the body mass of an animal and its brain mass is $y = 1.5196x + 61.585$. If the body mass increases by 1 kg, the brain mass **is likely to** increase by **approximately** 1.5196 grams.

5 This is indicated by the slight increase in the r value, which means the data is **marginally** closer to the trend line.

6 Because r is close to 1, if I substitute body size into my equation, I **should** be able to make accurate predictions for brain size.

ISBN: 9780170462297

7 This means that the model **may not be** applicable to animals smaller than a house mouse.
8 This data shows that if the body mass of a species increased by 5 kg, we would **expect** an increase in brain mass of 69 grams.

9 When working out an extrapolation, the second graph is **less suitable**.
10 This residual graph also **suggests** that the linear model **is likely to be** the most appropriate.
11 The best fit for the data **is** the exponential curve, with the equation $y = 103.79\ e^{-0.017x}$.
12 r = 0.95, so my prediction **is likely to be** reliable.
13 I **cannot** be certain that this extrapolated value is accurate because I **cannot** assume that the trend will continue.
14 The equation $y = -0.9578x + 16.611$ describes the relationship between a child's age (x) and the length of time taken (y) to do a puzzle. The relationship **is** negative.

Pick the errors (p. 63)

1 'So this means' is incorrect. Separately these two bits of information may be correct but linked together makes this statement wrong.
2 What kind of relationship? And how strong is it?
3 Both graphs should be accurate images of the data. The polynomial graph fits the data better than the linear graph.
4 An r value of 0.38 does not mean there is no relationship. It means the relationship is weak. The trend is indicated by the equation of the line of best fit, not r.
5 'Extreme' doesn't describe why it's unusual. Compare its body mass and brain mass in relation to the rest of the data.
6 'Which means' is incorrect. Separately these two bits of information may be correct but linked together makes this statement wrong.
7 The equation of the trend line is used to calculate a prediction, so, if calculated correctly, it is always on the trend line. Your confidence in a prediction should be determined by its fit and position compared with the data.
8 A graph won't show how they affect one another but it may suggest there is a relationship between the two variables. If two variables are correlated, you cannot assume that one variable has an effect on the other variable.
9 Language too strong. We don't know the figures are correct, but if the model fits well, then predictions are likely to be accurate.

Practice tasks (pp. 68–79)

Practice task one (pp. 68–69)

1 The question implies a relationship, has no context, and one of the units is wrong.
Is there a relationship between fat (g) and energy (kJ) in Megabun's fast food, and if so, what is its nature?
2 Variables in the wording are the wrong way around — on the graph Total fat is the explanatory variable and Energy is the response variable. The graph is the sensible way round as the fat in the food item is likely to explain the amount of energy.
I am using fat as the explanatory variable and energy as the response variable.
3 Trend described incorrectly.
This suggests as the total fat increases, the energy levels increase.
4 There is one unusual point at (11.5, 2240). This product has a high level of kJ for the amount of fat.
5 The r value is not 52.355, it is 0.88471.
6 Constant in the equation used to calculate the rate of increase rather than the gradient.
The gradient tells us that for an increase of 1 gram of fat, we would expect to see an increase of 52.355 kJ of energy.
7 They have subtracted the constant rather than added it. A product with 20 g of fat should have 1561.58 kJ of energy.

Practice task two (pp. 70–74)

Research:

The rate of alcohol absorption can be affected by things such as body weight, gender, amount of food in a person's stomach and the amount of body fat. https://www.health.govt.nz/your-health/healthy-living/addictions/alcohol-and-drug-abuse/alcohol/effects-alcohol#:~:text=brain%20%E2%80%93%20brain%20damage%2C%20tremors%2C,changes%2C%20cirrhosis%20and%20liver%20failure

Breath testing is used as a screening tool, and can be used for evidential purposes. Often a blood test is administered to check accuracy or if drivers refuse a breath test. https://www.alcohol.org.nz/alcohol-you/drinking-and-driving

The breathalyser limit for drivers aged 20 and over in New Zealand is 250 mcg/L breath. If you are under 20, the limit is zero. https://www.transport.govt.nz/common-transport-queries/drink-driving-limits-in-new-zealand/#:~:text=Query%20Information,millilitres%20(ml)%20of%20blood.&text=You%20must%20not%20drive%20if,or%20blood%20exceeds%20these%20limits.

Question:

Is there a relationship between the volume of beer drunk (mL) by male university students during a two-hour period and their breathalyser reading (mcg alcohol/L of breath) and if so, what is its nature?

ISBN: 9780170462297

Variables:
Explanatory variable: volume of beer drunk during two hours (mL)
Response variable: Breathalyser reading (mcg alcohol/L of breath)
Reason for choice: The volume of beer drunk will definitely affect the breathalyser reading, and also, the volume of beer drunk is easily measured, but not everybody has a breathalyser. Therefore the relationship could be used to estimate the amount of alcohol in the breath from the volume of beer drunk.
Purpose:
This data could be useful for male students who don't have access to a breathalyser. They could use it to estimate the amount of alcohol in their system.
Features:
There is a strong positive, reasonably linear relationship between volume of beer drunk and breathalyser reading. This means that as the volume of beer drunk increases, the higher the breathalyser reading will be. There don't appear to be any significant unusual points.
Describe nature:
There is a strong positive linear relationship between the volume of beer drunk and the breathalyser reading. This means that students who have drunk more beer tend to have higher breathalyser readings. On average, an increase in 100 mL of alcohol consumed is likely to lead to an increase in breathalyser reading of 35.587 mcg/L.
Describe and justify strength:
I think that the relationship is strong because most points lie fairly close to the line of best fit. However, the scatter is not even. The points for those who have drunk less alcohol lie closer to the line of best fit than those for students who have drunk more alcohol.
The strong relationship is supported by an r value of 0.91197.
Prediction(s):
Extrapolation: A student who has drunk 2 L of beer in a two-hour period is likely to have a breathalyser reading of about 600 (600.71) mcg/L. We cannot have great confidence in this extrapolation because the linear trend may not continue, and the data points for higher volumes of beer drunk are quite widely scattered.
Interpolation: A student who has drunk 1 L of beer in a two-hour period is likely to have a breathalyser reading of about 245 (244.84) mcg/L. I am confident that this figure is reasonably accurate because it lies in the middle of several quite close data points.
Conclusion:
There is a positive linear relationship between the quantity of beer drunk by male students during a two-hour period and their breathalyser readings. The quantity of beer drunk could be used as a predictor for breath alcohol content for quantities below about one litre. However, for larger amounts of alcohol, prediction of breathalyser readings are not likely to be accurate.

The study could be improved by repeating it with a lot more people, recording the body mass of students in order to find out how much difference that makes, controlling the timing of the drinking within the two hours, investigating drinking for different periods of time, trying the same study with female students, etc.

Practice task three (pp. 75–79)
Price paid for the machine against time spent during the previous week.
Research:
A number of people look to purchase fitness equipment to use at home. This reduces the need to go to a gym and pay for membership fees. There are choices to purchase and hire with a number of companies. https://www.elitefitness.co.nz/
Is it worth buying a machine or is it a waste of money? https://www.bbc.com/worklife/article/20150413-is-a-home-gym-worth-it
Question:
Is there a relationship between the price paid for a fitness machine ($) and the length of time (hours) spent using it over the past week, and if so, what is its nature?
Explanatory variable: Price paid for the machine ($).
Response variable: Length of time (hours) spent using the machine over the previous week.
Reason for choice: I would like to know if the price paid for a machine can be used to predict how much a person uses it.
Purpose:
This information may help someone who is looking to purchase an exercise machine to see how much time people spend on their machines after purchasing it. This might help them to set a budget of how much they are willing to pay given the amount of time they will spend on it. Or whether hiring a machine is more sensible.
Features:
There is a fairly weak positive realtionship between the price paid for a fitness machine and the time spent using it. There appears to be an unusual point, (6500, 9.25). This person spent more money than most people on a machine, $6500, and spent a considerable amount of time on it in one week, 9.25 hours.
Describe nature:
There is a moderately strong positive relationship between the price paid for a fitness machine and the time spent using it during the previous week. This means that people who spend more on fitness machine tend to spend more time using it. On average, an increase in $1000 is likely to lead to an increase in 1.1 (1.0886) hours on the machine.
Describe and justify strength:
I think the relationship between price and usage of fitness machines is moderately strong because there are a few points close to the line, although others are a distance from the line of best fit. The moderately strong relationship is supported by an r value of 0.56267.

ISBN: 9780170462297

Prediction(s):
I predict that a person who pays $2000 is likely to spend about 5 (5.0144) hours per week using their machine.

Conclusion: There is a moderately strong relationship between the price paid for a fitness machine ($) and the length of time (hours) spent using it over the past week. This means that people who spend more on fitness machines tend to spend more time using them. However, there were only 32 pieces of data in this study, so its findings may not be reliable. It could be improved by surveying larger numbers of people who have bought fitness machines over the last three years.

Length of time the machine has been owned against time spent during the previous week.

Research:
A number of people look to purchase fitness equipment to use at home. This reduces the need to go to a gym and pay for membership fees. There are choices to purchase and hire with a number of companies. https://www.elitefitness.co.nz/
Is it worth buying a machine or is it a waste of money? https://www.bbc.com/worklife/article/20150413-is-a-home-gym-worth-it

Question:
Is there a relationship between how long the person has owned the machine (months) and the length of time (hours) spent using it over the past week, and if so, what is its nature?

Explanatory variable: Length of time they had owned the machine (months).

Response variable: Length of time (hours) spent using the machine over the previous week.

Reason for choice: I would like to know if how long a person has owned a machine can be used to predict how much the person uses it.

Purpose:
This information may help someone who is looking to purchase an exercise machine to see how much time people spend on their machines after purchasing it. This might help them to set a budget of how much they are willing to pay given the amount of time they will spend on it. Or whether hiring a machine is more sensible.

Features
There is a strong negative relationship between the length of time a fitness machine has been owned and the time spent using it during the previous week. There is one unusual point, (15, 8.5). This person has had the machine for 15 months and has used it for 8.5 hours in the previous week. This is more use than others who have had their machines for a similar amount of time. There are also a few people who in a short period of ownership have used their machines for more than 7 hours a week.

Describe nature:
There is a strong negative relationship between the length of time a fitness machine has been owned and the time spent using it during the previous week. This means that people who have owned a fitness machine for longer tend to spend less time using it. On average, an increase in 10 months of ownership is likely to lead to a reduction of use of 1.6 (1.593) hours per week.

Describe and justify strength:
I think the relationship between ownership and time used is strong because most of the points are fairly close to the trend line. This is supported by an r value of –0.7035.

Prediction(s):
I predict that a person who has owned their machine for 20 months is likely to spend about 3.5 (3.4845) hours per week using their machine.

Conclusion: There is a strong negative relationship between the how long a fitness machine has been owned (months) and the length of time (hours) spent using it over the past week. This means that people who have owned fitness machines for longer tend to spend less time using them. However, there were only 32 pieces of data in this study, so its findings may not be reliable. It could be improved by surveying larger numbers of people who have bought fitness machines over the last three years.

ISBN: 9780170462297